How To Rear Children

BY

DR. JACK HYLES

Pastor
First Baptist Church
Hammond, Indiana

HYLES-ANDERSON PUBLISHERS
HAMMOND, INDIANA

FOREWORD

Recently while visiting southern California and preaching twice daily in the Central Baptist Church of Pamona, California, in the greater Los Angeles area, I was riding down the freeway with Pastor Batema when the conversation suddenly turned toward the rearing of boys. For several minutes I spoke with Pastor Batema concerning what I think is the proper way to rear children. He suddenly looked at me with a serious countenance and said, "Dr. Hyles, you ought to publish those remarks. Why don't you write a book on rearing children?"

When I retired that evening my mind was fastened on his suggestion. I could not sleep until I had promised God that I would obey the command given to me through His servant, Pastor Batema, and put in print the ideas, philosophies, and methods that I believe are necessary in the rearing of children to become well-adjusted adults possessing character, integrity, and chastity.

This is not a textbook; it is a workbook. It is not exhaustive. Nevertheless, it is offered to you, dear reader, with a sincere prayer that it will help you to train up your child in the way that he should go.

MEET THE AUTHOR

Dr. Jack Hyles is a pastor, having pastored five churches over a period of a quarter of a century varying size from nineteen members to the 15,000-member First Baptist Church of Hammond, Indiana, where he has pastored for the past thirteen years.

Dr. Jack Hyles is an author. From his pen have come BLUE DENIM AND LACE, THE HYLES CHURCH MANUAL, THE HYLES SUNDAY SCHOOL MANUAL, STRENGTH AND BEAUTY, JACK HYLES' CHURCH BUS HANDBOOK, KISSES OF CALVARY, HOW TO BOOST YOUR CHURCH ATTENDANCE, LET'S GO SOUL WINNING, and other books and pamphlets.

Dr. Jack Hyles is an educator having served as President of the Baptist Bible College in Denver, Colorado, and more recently has founded the Hyles - Anderson Bible College near Hammond, Indiana.

Dr. Jack Hyles is a radio preacher who is now heard on approximately 70 radio stations from coast to coast in most of the large metropolitan centers in America.

Dr. Jack Hyles is a traveler. He flies over 100,000 miles each year to most of the fifty states speaking before pastors' groups in Bible conferences, conferences on revival and soul winning, conventions, Sunday school clinics, etc.

In this volume Dr. Jack Hyles is a counselor. The reader will feel that he is in Dr. Hyles' study listening to him as he, in a conversational way, counsels with parents exhorting and training them to train up their children in the way that they should go.

TABLE OF CONTENTS

Chapter One

DEVELOPING THE WILL

"He that is slow to anger is better than the mighty; and he that ruleth his spirit than he that taketh a city."

—Proverbs 16:32

A paraphrase of the above Scripture would be, "Who is the hero? The hero is the man who restrains himself." Supreme in the rearing of a child is the developing of character. It is more important for a child to *be* what he ought to *be* than to do what he ought to do or know what he ought to know. If the child *is* what he ought to *be,* he will *do* what he ought to *do* and learn what he ought to know. In our generation the cultivating of the intellect is thought to be the answer; consequently, the child is taught, school is emphasized, and higher education is considered imperative. To be sure, the intellect is a part of the mind. There is, however, another part of the mind that is far too often overlooked — the will. For the intellect to be trained and the will to be untrained is dangerous. Susanna Wesley said she disciplined each of her children until his will was broken. The wise parent starts when the child is an infant in the training of the will.

The training of the will means the child is taught to do right by constant practice so that the mind rises to action by reflex just like the body. When the will has been brought into subjection to do that which is right the child learns to make his decisions by mental reflex. This is accomplished by applying a certain

9

stimulus to the child and having him practice the proper response. For example, when I was a boy my mother used to have me practice standing when a lady would walk into the room. I would be seated; Mother would go outside and reenter. As she entered I would stand. She would go out again; I would sit down again. She would enter again; I would stand again. Over and over this was repeated until it became almost a reflex for me to stand when a lady entered a room. This was continued day by day until I never had to decide to stand when a lady entered the room. I stood by mental reflex. Hour after hour Mother would practice with me on giving a lady my seat when there were no other seats available. I would sit down and Mother would walk out of the room. She would reenter. I would stand and say, "Ma'am, would you like my seat?" She would sit down. This was done over and over and over again until it was a subconscious thing for me to rise and offer a lady my seat.

It is only logical to assume that the more things a person does the more chances he has to do something wrong. Hence, the more decisions one has to make during a day the more likely he is to make the wrong decisions and the more wrong decisions he is likely to make. Consequently, if one lets his principles make his decisions for him, he will make fewer mistakes and yes, commit fewer sins. This means that one decides what he will always do under any given stimulus or circumstance and this is practiced until it becomes part of the subconscious. He will have spared himself the temptation of facing a decision each time a certain stimulus or a certain circumstance confronts him. Hence, one's principles will make his decisions and he decides only once and for all what the principles will be.

Luther Burbank said that you can fix a desired

trait in a human being by constant practice like you can fix a desired trait in a plant.

This is done only by constant practice. Recently I was entertaining a famous preacher. I was driving when suddenly we came to a stoplight that was changing. I jammed on the brakes and threw my right hand in front of the preacher. He grinned and asked what I was doing. I laughed and said I was trying to keep the baby from hitting the dash as the car stopped abruptly. Now "the baby" is married and has a baby of her own; yet after all these years the subconscious caused me to try to protect the baby. I had done it so often that by reflex I jammed the brakes and threw my hand in front of the famous preacher.

Recently on a given Sunday I baptized over 100 people. When I baptize a convert I raise my right hand in the air and say the following words: "In obedience to the command of our Lord and Master, and upon a public profession of your faith in Him, I baptize you, my brother (or sister), in the name of the Father, the Son, and the Holy Spirit. Amen." I said those words over 100 times. After the service I went home. The phone rang. I picked up the receiver with my right hand, but every time I had raised my right hand that morning I had said, "In obedience to the command, etc." When I used my right hand to raise the phone to my ear I said, "In obedience to the command of our Lord and Master, and upon a public profession of your faith in Him, I baptize you, my brother, in the name of the Father, the Son. . ." Then I realized what I was doing. By reflex after practice I said those words when I raised my right hand.

Not long ago I was going to go to the store. It is only four blocks from my house. I got in the car but was thinking about church work, etc., so naturally I found myself driving into my parking place at the

First Baptist Church. I had driven three or four miles along the usual route that I take to the church and did not realize where I was going until I was sitting in front of the church. I have taken that route so much that when the subconscious took over I ended up at the church, not at the store.

I take natural vitamins and minerals. I keep several jars of vitamins in a drawer in my office. From the first bottle of vitamins I take four tablets a day. From the second bottle, which contains vitamin E, I take two tablets a day. One day I opened the drawer and did not realize that the vitamin E was in the wrong place. It was first in line. By force of habit, I took four vitamin E tablets (which, by the way, is not a good idea). The subconscious had taken over. I had taken four tablets of the first bottle for so long that I didn't notice which bottle was in the first position.

The above illustrations show how the will can be trained to react by reflex. This is good only if we teach our children the proper good reaction to certain stimuli until the decisions of life are made by mental reflex and good is done subconsciously. This means the child will do right by habit, for basically, character is learning the proper habits. It is learning to do right without voluntary action. It is the subconscious doing of right. This can be done only by practice and more practice and more practice.

The wise parent will make a list of the things he wants his child to do under certain conditions and influences. He will then require the child to practice the proper response to each condition and stimulus. When my children were little I made a list of all the things I wanted them to learn to do by mental reflex. Some of these things were: answering the phone properly, shaking hands properly, walking, sitting, using correct posture, paying bills, having respect for elders, and many others. Each evening we would spend some time practicing each of these things until they became natural. This is the way a child learns to walk, to eat, etc. This is the way an athlete learns to be successful.

When I was a child my mother would often ask me this question, "Son, would you like a cigarette?" I would say, "No!" She would ask me again, "Would you like a cigarette?" I would say, "No!" Over and over again she would ask the same question and I would give the same answer. She was trying to get me to associate the word "NO" with cigarettes. She did the same thing about liquor and other temptations. She would hold up cigarette ads in front of me and say, "No, no, no, no, no, no, no, no, no!" Then she would ask me to do the same thing. I would look at the cigarette ad and say, "No, no, no, no, no, no, no, no!" until the two words "cigarette" and "no" became associated indelibly in my subconscious mind.

Every great nation, whether her philosophies were right or wrong, rose to greatness using this method of teaching. Such discipline made America a great nation. She is now crumbling because of the lack of it. All strong nations were made strong by such training of the will. Such programs had been added to their schools. Every nation that has crumbled did so when such discipline was deserted.

The wise parent, the wise pastor, the wise coach, etc. will produce the proper decisions by constant repetition until the child has learned to do right without voluntary action. Hence, the will has been cultivated to make decisions by principle. The making of decisions by the child, or the adult for that matter, will have less chance of being wrong when the doing of right has become habit!

Chapter Two

THE IMPORTANCE OF SELF-CONTROL

In the previous chapter we found that the developing of the proper character is the supreme part of rearing a child. Now the most important part of developing the right character is the developing of self-control. Self-control is the will conquering attention. It is the appetite being satisfied only when the will allows. It is the will conquering the appetite rather than the appetite conquering the will.

When children are infants we often place things over their cribs such as little birds that move about with the slightest wind. The child's attention is captured by these little birds. His will is a slave to his attention. He does not decide at what he will look. He looks at that thing which is most attractive to him. In other words, he is affected by an external stimulus. Self-control comes when the will takes over and decides what a person does. His actions are decided by his will rather than by the appeal to the senses. Unless self-control is developed a person will decide to do in life whatever is most attractive and most pleasant. This, of course, leads to shipwreck.

A person walks down the street and smells popcorn. He cannot resist. His appetite decides what he eats. The attractiveness of the popcorn on the outside has made his decision for him. The disciplined person eats popcorn only when he needs it. His will controls his appetite. He decides what he looks at; he decides what he eats; he decides where he goes; he has control of himself. He is not a slave to appetites, pleasures, and passions.

How can one train a child to exercise such self-control? This is done by developing something on the inside that becomes more attractive than that which is on the outside. Then more pleasure is gotten inwardly by resistance than outwardly by yielding. For example, my son, David, is an athlete. During basketball season he does not drink carbonated drinks nor eat pastry. This is not to say that chocolate pie is not attractive. Quite to the contrary, it is most attractive, but there is something on the inside that is more attractive — the satisfaction of making the team, of being in good condition, and of pleasing the coach! Hence, the inward pleasure has overcome the competitive attractiveness of external pleasure. He has developed self-control. His will decides whether or not he eats chocolate pie. Hence, in this matter he is in control of himself. He is not a beast; he is a man. He derives more pleasure inwardly by not eating the chocolate pie than he would derive outwardly by eating it.

As the parent develops such self-control within the child he must make the inward attractiveness so great that it is worth the hurt of being deprived the satisfying of the appetite. The pleasure of self-control must be greater than the pleasure of indulgence. If this can be done, the person is in control of his body rather than a slave to it.

One must then seek to find these things that can be more appealing. *One is that of a goal.* Lead the child to have in his mind the pleasure of attaining a certain goal. Teach him to let nothing stop him in attaining this desired end. For example, suppose a boy is saving to buy a new bicycle. The wise parent will remind him over and over again of the desired goal so that no immediate appetite can rise up and capture some of his money. He continues to save toward this end even when the county fair comes to town. The boy looks at the county fair. He finds it so appealing to the outside that it competes with the inner desire to save for a bicycle. If he is trained properly, he will not sacrifice the reaching of the desired goal for a brief pleasure. The child should be led to have in his mind the pleasure of attaining a goal, and this internal satisfaction should be greater to him than the appeal from the sight of the bright lights, the smell of good food, etc. of the county fair.

Another internal competition is that of punishment. Punishment for wrong-doing is a necessary and vital part of rearing a child and developing his character. The punishment should always hurt more than the pleasure feels good. For example, a young man stays out thirty minutes late with his girlfriend and all he gets is a scolding or a spanking. Now what young man wouldn't be willing to trade a spanking for thirty minutes with a lovely girl! The wise parent will take the car away from the boy, ground him, and not let him be with his girlfriend for one week. Hence, he is trading an entire week for thirty minutes. This is not a good trade and he will be on time henceforth, for the punishment has brought more displeasure than the offense brought pleasure. In the mind of the boy that particular appetite will always have associated with it the punishment that was inflicted.

It might be wise for the parent to list the different appetites from which he wants his child to refrain. He then should make very plain to the child what the punishment is so the child will know whether or not refraining will be worth it.

I once had a black cat who loved to jump on the bathroom stove and put her paws in the lavatory while I shaved. Winter came and the stove was turned on. The black cat jumped up on the stove! In fact, the cat kept on jumping, and never again did she get on the stove! Even in summertime she would look at the stove with suspicion but she would never chance it. The joy of watching me shave was not great enough for the chance she would have to take. This may be transferred into a child's subconscious until the fear of punishment will be so great that the attractiveness of the wrong will be lessened.

Another internal competitor to outward attractions is that of pleasing and/or not hurting someone who cares. Here is a very strong internal pleasure or displeasure. If a close relationship can be developed between the parents and the child, the child will have an intense desire to please them. If he feels much displeasure and pain when he displeases Mom and Dad, then the external attraction will be limited by the thought of pleasing those he loves. When I was a boy in grade school my report cards were marked either "S" for satisfactory, "U" for unsatisfactory, or "N" for needs improvement. "N" was neither real good nor real bad. One time I came home with an "N" in conduct. My mother cried and cried and cried. You would have thought I had fallen into some terrible sin. Lamentation and tears filled the house. During the next grading period every time I would start to whisper to the boys around me I could see my weeping mother and I would be a good boy. With that picture in my mind I worked hard for the entire period and sure enough, I received an "S" for satisfactory in conduct. When I brought the "S" home she was so happy she danced for joy and jumped with glee. You would have thought I had discovered a cure for leukemia. She made it such a big thing that when I was tempted to misbehave in school I could see her both rejoicing and sorrowing. The desire to see her pleased overcame the desire to talk to the boy behind me. Hence, the attractiveness of the internal feeling exceeded the attractiveness of the external stimulus and I became a pretty good kid.

Still another of these competitors against external pleasantness is the desire for praise. This is an important factor in rearing children. It is vital, however, that the parents praise character, not talent! It is more important that a child be praised for being punctual than for singing a song and that he be praised more for being honest or working hard than for displaying some talent. Character properly praised can do much to give the child control over his will so that he decides what appetites he fills and when he fills them.

The following paragraphs will list some general statements concerning self-control.

1. *The child should be taught not to sacrifice a present good for a permanent one.* Reference was previously made to a child's saving to buy a bicycle. The county fair came along and he faced a present pleasure versus a future pleasure. The word "no" should immediately have popped into his mind. Yes, the excitement and pleasures of the county fair are many, but there are many more pleasures spread over many months if he refrains and continues to save for the bicycle. As Dr. Bob Jones, Sr. used to say, "Never sacrifice the future on the altar of the present."

2. *The child should not be punished because he displeases the parents nor should he be rewarded simply on the basis of the parents' pleasure.* In other words, the parent should not be guilty of the same offense from which he is trying to wean the child. The offense is that of responding because of external pleasure. This does not mean the child should not try to please the parent. It simply means that the reward should come because of the child's disciplining his will, and the punishment should come because the child does wrong. Children are often punished for restlessness as if it were an offense of the will. The

mother who says to a child, "I am sick and tired of hearing you cry," and punishes the child because she is sick and tired is acting unwisely. Just as the child is being trained to use his will instead of external pleasures, so the wise parent will use his will in the punishment of a child and not external pleasures or displeasures derived from the child's behaviour.

3. *The child should be taught that "ought" and "can" are synonymous.* Someone has said, "You can do what you ought to do." Emerson wrote, "So nigh is grandeur to our dust, so near is God to man, when duty whispers, 'Lo thou must,' the youth replies, 'I can.' " This is just another way to say that the wise young person is taught that he can do what he ought to do.

My mother used to have me repeat the following three words over and over again, "I ought, I can, I will. I ought, I can, I will. I ought, I can, I will. I ought, I can, I will." Charles Sumner said, "Three things are necessary for success: first, backbone; second, backbone; third, backbone." An old proverb says, "Kites ride against the wind, not with the wind." Another says, "Only dead fish float with the stream; live ones swim against it."

4. *Children should be taught to say, "No!"* A child should stand in front of the mirror and practice saying "no" in many ways.

Gertrude Atherton wrote the novel, RULER OF KINGS. In it a rich man sent his boy to be reared in a poor home. The person rearing him required the boy to say "no" twenty times the first thing in the morning and twenty times the last thing at night.

Plutarch said that the people of Asia became vassals largely because they could not say "no."

My mother would get a bottle, put water in it, and pretend it was an alcoholic beverage. She then would

say to me, "Son, would you like a bottle of beer?"
My answer was to be an emphatic "NO!" Again she
would say, "Son, how about a bottle of beer?" I would
answer, "No!" Then she would say, "Son, do
you want some wine?" My answer was "no." She
would repeat the aforementioned questions many
times so that later in life when I was really offered
liquor I had associated the word "no" with beer,
whiskey, wine, etc. so long that I would again say
"No!" She did the same thing with cigarettes. She
would pretend that she had a package of cigarettes
and ask me if I would like to have one. I would say,
"No!" This was repeated many times. The wise
parent will list the things from which he wants his
child to refrain and will train the child to associate
the word "no" with this particular thing. My mother
would hold up a liquor ad and say, "No, no, no, no,
no, no, no." She would then tear it up, throw it on
the floor, and stomp on it, all the time saying, "No,
no, no, no, no, no." She would then give me a liquor
ad. I would say, "No, no, no, no, no, no." Then I
would tear it up, throw it on the floor and stomp on
it saying, "No, no, no, no, no, no."

5. *Children should be taught not to let the crowd
influence them in any direction.* Many fine parents
have taught their children not to run with the crowd
and their motives are good ones. This, however, is not
a good, hard and fast rule. It would be better for the
child to be taught not to let the crowd influence him
either way. Theodore Munger said, "Suspect the
crowd, resist it." The first part of that statement is
unquestionably right. The last part is not always a
good criterion. Suppose the crowd is going to church.
Suppose the crowd is not drinking. Hence, it seems
that it would be better for the child to be taught that
he should not go because the crowd goes nor stay
because the crowd stays. He should hold the scales

of right and wrong in his own hands and should decide what he does by his will. When a person refuses to go with the crowd just because the crowd is going, he is not acting from his own will. Again an external stimulus is motivating him. The crowd should have nothing to do with his decision.

Someone has said, "When I assent without thought to what another person says, when I do as he wishes without reasoning for myself, there is but one person present; I am nobody."

I have said to my son many times, "Son, be your own man. Do not let the crowd influence you either way." Though it is true that the crowd is usually wrong, and the Christian is often in the minority, it is not always the case. There will be times when a child is going to be with good Christian people and it would be wrong to refrain from what they are doing. The basis of judgment, however, should be on the matter of right and wrong, not who is doing it.

6. *Teach the child not to fear unpopularity.* It is not what others will think of me, but what I will think of myself. One should not fear being unpopular with others, but being unpopular with himself.

7. *The parents should be consistent with punishment.* The same offense should be punished in the same way so the child can learn a pattern of behavior. Suppose little Johnny stayed five minutes too long at Billy's house and his mother says, "Johnny, you can't play with Billy now for two days." Then the next time Johnny is late from Billy's house he should receive the same punishment, so it is registered in his mind that five minutes too much time with Billy will cause him to forfeit two days with Billy. Hence, the same offense has the same punishment. Johnny will be able to learn a pattern of behavior by knowing what the punishment is for each offense. Years ago I sat down and listed the most

common offenses committed by the children. I then listed the punishment that I felt each offense warranted. After months of receiving the same punishment for each offense, the children began to associate certain wrongs with certain types of punishment which allowed them to weigh the price subconsciously before committing the crime. Far too many children do not know what the price is. One time the parent will spank a child for a particular wrong. The next time the child is sent to his room; the next time he is scolded for the same offense. Perhaps later the parent will overlook it completely until in the mind of the child there is developed a willingness to gamble, "Maybe this will be the time that Mom will do nothing or simply give me a lecture." When tempted he is often willing to chance it, for there is always that possibility that he will get by with it. If, however, he knew that without exception he would pay a certain penalty, and if that penalty brought more discomfort and displeasure than the wrong brought pleasure, he would realize there was not a chance in the world that he could get by without being punished. This leads to another very important thing in child rearing.

8. *Always make the pain of the punishment far in excess of the pleasure of the wrong:* For example, a boy comes in thirty minutes late from a date. He could have gotten home on time but he wanted to spend thirty minutes more with his girlfriend. He is scolded or maybe even spanked. Now what boy wouldn't be willing to get a spanking for thirty minutes more with his girlfriend? What boy wouldn't be willing to get a lecture in exchange for thirty extra exciting minutes? In such a case the parent might well forbid the boy from seeing his girlfriend for a week. When this punishment is meted out consistently for this offense, the boy will realize that he will always have to trade

an entire week for thirty minutes if he stays out too late.

In the aforementioned punishment there is also another important observation that should be made. The punishment should often involve the withdrawal of the thing which has been done in excess. In other words, the son should not be refused permission to be with a boyfriend for a week. Most teenage boys would be glad to trade a week with a boyfriend for thirty minutes with a girlfriend, but grounding him from seeing the girl will hit him where it hurts and will do him more good.

9. *Punishment should not be given because the parent is annoyed, but rather, because right has been offended and wrong has been committed.* In other words, the child should not be punished because of personality weaknesses, but rather because of character weaknesses. Far too many of us demonstrate the opposite of what we are teaching! We teach our children to be motivated by the will rather than by external stimuli, but then we punish them strictly on the basis of external stimuli, such as when we are annoyed with their actions, etc.

10. *Self-control in eating should be strongly emphasized from infancy.* Parents are largely to blame for the appetites of their children. Instead of providing food on the basis of nourishing the body, building up tissue, supplying energy, etc., they supply food highly spiced that provokes appetite instead of satisfying it. Such food makes the child sluggish and dull instead of active, healthy, and vigorous. Hence, the child is taught he should eat what tastes good instead of what is good for him. If a family overfeeds a valuable horse, they are considered cruel. The purpose of food is to nourish the body. When eating is done just for the pleasure that results from the gratification of taste, the end is overeating. Overeating

causes the body to perform its functions poorly and causes the person to be a slave to his appetites. The Apostle Paul reminds us in I Corinthians 10:31 that whatever we eat should be to the glory of God.

Breeders of fine horses and dogs pay more attention to proper feeding than the average mother does for her children. Chickens are fed more carefully than children. From early childhood a child should be taught self-control in eating. He should be taught that the purpose of eating is to make the body healthy. Eating is to the body what filling the tank with gasoline is to the car. The body will run no better than its fuel allows. One does not buy gasoline for his car according to how it smells or how pretty it is; he buys it according to the performance it gives to the car. This same rule should apply to our bodies.

There is more, however, to the control of one's appetite than health alone. The desire for food is one of the few appetites that are developed early in life. Hence, if a child is taught self-control concerning eating, he will become master of his own will, and when other appetites are developed he will be able to exercise self-control in them also by transferring the character he has developed into other areas of temptation. Why not feed the child apples, grapes, oranges, etc. instead of candy; fruit juices instead of carbonated drinks; nuts, such as almonds and pecans, in the place of "snick-snacks"? Good food can be as delicious to the child as bad food, and proper diet can be as tasty as improper diet if the parent leads the child to develop tastes for that which is healthy and nourishing.

11. *The will should control the temper.* Controlling the temper means that one's will prevents expression of his inner feelings and thereby prevents reaction. Anger should be allowed or disallowed by the will. It is not wrong to become angry; however, it

is wrong to become angry because we are annoyed or because we have been wronged. Usually our anger does not come from a hatred of wrong, but because we think we have been wronged. Hence, it comes from outside stimuli and this is why we "fly off the handle." Children should be taught to hate injustice and wrong. They must learn to be angry not because they have been wronged, but because someone whom they love has done wrong. Oftentimes a person who exhibits his temper will make such statements as, "I just get it off my chest and get it over with." This sounds very good but the truth is, it simply makes it easier for passion to follow the same path and to seek the same relief the next time he is offended. Hence, a habit is formed because the person has given way to anger.

One reason anger is so deadly is that it defeats the one who is angry rather than the one who is the object of the anger. Someone said to me recently, "I was so mad I didn't know what I was doing." Such uncontrollable temper leads to murder, bad health, broken friendships, and perhaps worst of all, the breakdown of self-control which may be transferred into other areas until restraint is almost impossible and anger is an automatic reaction which divorces a person's actions from his will. Because of this a child should be taught to count to ten before he gives in to his feelings, for the time that is gained in counting to ten or in the thought of the ritual gives opportunity to reason before hasty action takes place. It gives the will time to collect itself in order to gain supremacy over the reaction. The wise man said, "A soft answer turneth away wrath." Another has said, "Govern your passions or they will govern you." Franklin said, "What error is begun in anger ends in shame." Jefferson said, "When angry count ten; when very angry, one-hundred."

12. *Children should be taught to finish a task.*
Each job should be done completely and well. Never
should the parent finish the task for the child. No
food should be left on the plate and no satisfaction
should be allowed for a job that goes unfinished.
Napoleon once said, "Impossible is a word found
only in the dictionary of fools." Hence, a task that is
begun should be finished regardless of how difficult it
is. The child who is allowed to let another finish a job
that he starts does not develop self-control and later
is found bouncing from one job to another, one
school to another, etc.

This is especially true when a task is an unpleasant
one. Teach him to fix his mind on the goal. Teach
him the joy of accomplishing the goal and finishing
the task. Teach him the shame of a task unfinished.
Let him understand that he is being conquered when
he does not finish an unpleasant task. Let the joy of
doing a job well overcome the drudgery of the work
itself.

I know one parent who listed all of the tasks that
were unpleasant to his child. The parent led the child
to call the tasks "Goliath" and himself "David." The
child was taught to get angry at the tasks and refuse
to be conquered by Goliath. When the child
conquered a task the parent praised him, as David was
praised when he defeated Goliath.

Hence, work should be a challenge and
perseverance should be a habit. This would teach the
child to work hard, which in essence is a fruit of
self-control. Fortunate is the child who is made to
work hard.

My Uncle Harvey, who passed away several years
ago, was a wealthy man. He had one son whom he
required to mow yards and do other hard tasks of labor
in order to get spending money. Unwise critics would
look and say, "Poor son! There is that mean old father

with all that money who makes his boy work so hard."
Wise people, however, would say, "What a fortunate
son to have a father who realizes what makes
character!" He was giving his son more than money. He
was teaching him habits, perseverance, the need for
hard work, and other attributes that made much
money for the son in later years.

In summary, character is habit and habit is formed
by practice. When Becky, David, Linda, and Cindy
were little children I listed all of the things I wanted
them to do and do well. Such things as how to answer
the telephone properly, how to meet friends, how to
react when an adult enters the room, etc. were listed.
Each evening we would practice one of these things.
The boy would practice walking like a boy and the
girls would practice walking like girls. They would
practice sitting, standing, being graceful, being kind,
etc. We would act out a sample situation and repeat it
over and over again until certain reflexes would cause
the child to respond automatically to certain stimuli.
May God help us to teach our children to have
self-control.

Chapter Three

PROPER MANNERS

Someone has said, "Manners are the bridges which men build over the gulfs which separate them and their castles of self and over which they pass in their dealings with one another." Basically then the having of good manners is displaying the proper treatment, mingled with propriety, to one's fellowman. Better still, it is simply living by the golden rule. At the First Baptist Church of Hammond, Indiana, we stress one word to our young people above all other words. That word is "appropriate." We believe that education includes the ability to be appropriate in any given right situation without embarrassing one's fellowman. Our young people are taught to know and exhibit proper behavior whether on the ball field, at a concert, in church, out fishing, or at home with the family. This chapter will deal with the proper development of manners for our children toward their fellowman.

1. *Proper manners should be an appropriate outward expression of an inner feeling of goodwill toward our fellowman.* In other words, manners are an outward expression of an inner feeling. Manners are therefore more than ritual and form. There should be a friendly and brotherly feeling of sympathy and helpfulness toward others. Good manners are simply the expression of this inner condition of the mind. Improper manners are an expression of an improper frame of mind and attitude toward others. Hence, the first way to instill good manners in the child is to instill in his heart a feeling of brotherly kindness and

28

goodwill toward all human beings. This is brought about by possession of true Bible meekness. The word "meek" in the Bible implies "equality." A person who possesses true meekness says not, "I am as good as you are," but rather, "You are as good as I am." This philosophy should be the foundation of good manners, for when it is present, manners will take care of themselves.

Courtesy, then, becomes simply the expression of the state of one's mind. This is not to say we are not to be courteous if we do not have a mind to do so. We should exhibit courtesy even if it is mere form, but courtesy in its purest sense is when the proper behavior toward others expresses the proper attitude toward him. The courteous man says, "You are my equal and I have a friendly feeling toward you." The discourteous person says, "You are not my equal and I am not interested in you. I am interested only in myself." Manners become symbols which indicate without words a friendly disposition of one's mind toward his fellowman. When he shakes hands he is using an ancient custom which was brought about by the giving of one's right hand to another making his hand engaged so he would be unable to fight. It is the joining of two fighting hands and the voluntary giving of one's weapon in battle. Hence, it is a symbol which says, "I do not want to hit you. I do not want to fight you, for I feel friendly toward you."

In the early days when a warrior came to someone with whom he did not want to fight, he took off his helmet. Hence, we take off our hats today in the presence of a friend. This is to tell him, "I do not want to war with you and I feel so confidently that you do not want to war with me that I am willing to remove that which guards the safety of my head." Again, here is a symbol of the inner condition of one's heart.

2. *Proper manners will create this inner goodwill.*
It is somewhat like the hen and the egg. Each
reproduces the other. Our goal is for the child to have
the proper feeling toward others so as to generate
good manners. On the other hand, this proper feeling
is often created by good manners themselves. They
help produce the feeling for which they are the sign.
Put a sour look on one's face and in turn he will have
a sour feeling in his heart. Consequently, in a sense,
each man creates his own atmosphere. A smile on
one's face will soon put a smile in his heart. This is
one of the main reasons why proper dress is
important. How we dress and behave can determine
how we feel inwardly. In turn, how we feel inwardly
helps us dress and behave more properly.

3. *Proper manners should first be exhibited at
home.* This, of course, is because the habits are
formed at home. Children should be taught to say
happily, "Good morning," to those at home, to use
the word "please" when they ask a favor, to be
generous with the phrase, "thank you," and to be
unselfish, especially toward their parents. One of the
most important things in rearing a child to have good
manners is to teach that child to prefer his parents.
He should always be seeking the comfort and pleasure
of them, seeing to it that Mom and Dad get the most
comfortable chairs, their favorite positions, etc. Many
parents think this would be selfishness on their part,
which is not true at all! Their motive for teaching
their child this type of behavior is not so the parent
will enjoy life more but so that the child will exhibit
proper manners at home which will later be
transferred to those outside the home. Confuscius
said, "Eat at your own table as you would eat at the
table of the king."

Emphasis should be placed on proper manners at
the table in the child's home. He should learn to seat

himself properly, sit properly, wait until his turn to
be served, etc. He should be taught the proper way of
holding a fork, the placing of a napkin on his lap,
proper chewing of the food, and other basic manners
so often forgotten in our generation. He should not
be allowed to reach across the table. He should
refrain from expressions of dislike for certain foods.

These manners should be practiced. We have
learned that character is the developing of the proper
habits. The proper habits can be developed only
through practice. Much practice should be given
concerning proper table manners and home
courtesies.

One of the most important things a child should be
taught is to be cheerful at home since cheerfulness
and cleanliness are both contagious. We must be
careful to affect others properly with our
personalities. A child should be taught to laugh. (Of
course, this should also be done with propriety and
temperance.) Laughter makes one more healthy. It
causes the heart to beat faster and sends the blood
bounding through the body. When a person laughs,
respiration is increased, the eye brightens, the chest
expands, bad air is forces out of the lungs, the internal
organs are caused to vibrate, etc. Laughter
has a good effect on the liver and gastric juices. In
some cases physicians have prescribed laughter. One
doctor even gave a patient this prescription:
"Laughter to be taken five minutes every three
hours." A cheerful spirit at home will help to create a
proper state of mind and a proper state of mind can
create proper manners.

4. *Being punctual is one of the essentials for good
manners, for not being on time is one of the great
injustices that one human being can do to another.*
Lack of promptness and punctuality is really stealing.
It is stealing the other person's time. It is also lying,

for it is a failure to keep promises.

Napoleon was always ahead of time. He said, "Every moment lost is an opportunity for misfortune."Lord Nelson, the English admiral, said that his success was largely attributed to the fact that he was always on time. He said he gave himself a quarter of an hour extra time. This allowed for accidents.

Matthews said that men who are habitually behind time are habitually behind success. Napoleon said he beat the Austrians because they did not know the value of five minutes.

A man once spent some time in Benjamin Franklin's book shop. He was looking at a certain book and asked its price. The salesman replied that it cost $1. The customer asked to see Benjamin Franklin about the price. Although Franklin was very busy the man would not be satisfied until he was called. He then proceeded to tell Mr. Franklin how much he wanted the book, for what purpose, etc. and asked for the lowest price Mr. Franklin could place on the book. Franklin replied, "$1.25." The man was stunned and said, "All your clerk asked was $1."

"Yes," said Franklin, "but you have taken my time which is worth far more than a quarter." The man objected and finally asked again what the price was. Franklin replied. "The price is now $1.50 for you have taken more of my time." The man immediately paid the $1.50 and left the store.

Parents should constantly stress to their children the importance of promptness and punctuality. This is why churches should start their services on time. School teachers should stress thee importance of arriving in class on time, in order that the child may form habits of punctuality for his future life.

A child should get up on time, go to bed on time,

come home from school on time, and keep all of his
appointments. Promptness is doing the duty now. It
is doing a task on time. The mind should receive an
indelible impression of the time an appointment is to
be kept and it should be kept without fail.

5. *There are some definite manners that the parent
should practice and rehearse with the child:*

(1) Standing when an adult walks into the
room.

(2) Introducing one's self properly to a
stranger. For instance, Hyles is an unusual
name. I have found it best to spell it out
when I give my name to a stranger.

(3) Properly introducing one's friend to
another.

(4) Shaking hands. Young men should
especially spend much time practicing
shaking hands with attention given to a
firm handshake and to looking the person
in the eye while speaking.

(5) Walking. Girls should be taught to walk
like ladies and boys should be taught to
walk like men.

(6) Sitting gracefully. Boys should be taught
to sit like men and girls should be taught
to sit like ladies.

(7) Answering the telephone. Something like,
"Good morning, this is Johnny Doe,"
would be appropriate. Perhaps some
families would prefer, "This is the Doe
residence; Johnny is speaking."

(8) The giving of a seat by a young man to a
lady.

(9) Using proper table manners.

(10) Not interrupting another who is speaking.

(11) Showing courtesy to strangers, aged

people, and guests.

(12) Respecting age and showing preference to one's elders.

(13) Avoiding slang and profane speech. The use of slang implies that one goes along with the crowd as they are affected by the desire to be popular. It implies that one is not a strong personality, that his vocabulary is very limited, and that he does not have the proper words at his command to express his meaning properly. It implies the lack of will power. It implies the lack of mental maturity and propriety.

(14) Not complaining, grumbling, finding fault.

(15) Refraining from disturbing the enjoyment of others by talking loudly and laughing in public.

(16) Having personal dignity and self-respect.

(17) Exercising good manners in business. Professor Shaler of Harvard once said in "The Citizen" that his own observations show that more young men fail from lack of manners than from any other one cause.

My boy, David, was in want and in need of a summer job. There were simply no jobs available and there were many young men applying for each position. He went to apply for a certain construction job. Several young men were ahead of him, but surprisingly he was employed for the job. The employer said later that he decided to hire David when he shook his hand and introduced himself.

It is amazing and appalling how many people go to the bank to borrow money improperly dressed and with a crude kind of manners. Young men should be taught to wear suits and ties and proper clothing, to give their names properly, shake hands, and to present their business articulately.

(18) Behaving properly in public meetings.

(19) Using proper terms, such as "Thank you," "Please," "You're welcome," "Pardon me," "Excuse me," etc.

(20) Answering the door.

These and other manners and courtesies must not be taught once and forgotten. They must be repeated over and over again. They must be rehearsed and practiced until the child responds to each situation by reflex. Someone has said, "No one can disgrace us but ourselves." Carlyle once said, "Good breeding remembers the rights of others; low breeding insists upon one's own rights."

Once because I was kind to an old lady she gave to our church $14,000 for the purchase of two new buses. When I showed her kindness I had no idea she was a lady of means.

A family of ten was converted and joined my church because I made it a habit to wave at them as they drove by in a yellow car. Once a lady who was a stranger to me said that my laugh kept her from committing suicide.

In this day when an arrogant, cocky, know-it-all manner seems to be popular, we should start early in the lives of our children in training them to feel properly toward their fellowmen and to express this feeling with proper manners. The word "appropriate" should be stressed over and over again and propriety should be practiced until the child is courteous and proper by instinct so as never to embarrass himself, his family, or his friends in any given proper and right situation.

Chapter Four

REVERENCE FOR GOD

God created man that He might have fellowship with him. When sin broke this fellowship God initiated a plan whereby it might be restored. No life is a success unless it has been used as a preparation for the next life. Regardless of the accomplishments a person makes, his life is a failure unless he is prepared for dying. Now what does this have to do with early childhood? Simply this: A child that is taught reverence for God when he is yet too young to understand the plan of redemption will quickly accept Christ when he is old enough to understand what it is all about. One of the great secrets to making this kind of an early response is to have developed in childhood a deep and an abiding reverence for God. The wise parent will prepare his child for acceptance of salvation and dedication of life by teaching him how to attain such reverence.

1. *He should be taught to respect all kinds of superiority, such as old age, skill, scholarship, parents, teachers, leaders, etc.* As he respects superiority, he will then by force of habit respect the greatest Superiority of all when he comes to understand what salvation is all about.

2. *He should be taught to have in his disciplined schedule a quiet time.* This is time he should spend alone talking to and thinking about God. This should be done at the same time every day and should be done without fail. He is developing a habit that will render him blessings and success in later life.

3. *He should be shown the universe and its*

grandeur.Read to him Psalms 8 and 19. Take him for a walk at night and show him the wonders and the immensity of the heavens. Teach him to say,

> "Twinkle, twinkle little star,
>   How I wonder what you are,
> Up above the world so high,
>   Like a diamond in the sky,"

Teach your child,

> "Star light, star bright,
>   First star I've seen tonight;
> I wish I may, I wish I might,
>   Have the wish I wish tonight."

Tell him that God made the heavens. Explain to him that most of those stars are bigger than our earth. Tell him how far away they are and how wonderful is God's universe. Teach him that God made the universe. Lead him to stand in awe over the greatness of God and the wonders of the heavens.

4. *He should be taught of the wonders of life.* Show him ants, bees, etc. who live in our world and yet, in a sense, who live each in his own world. Tell him of the ant, for example. Read in an encyclopedia some of the characteristics of the ant. Let the child become intrigued with the intelligence of some supreme being, even our God, Who made the wonders of nature. Teach him to believe in God because of the arrangement of God's world. This kind of reverence comes from knowledge rather than superstition. Realization of the wonder and beauty of God's world will lead the child to have reverence for the Creator. Show him the plants in the spring and the trees in the autumn. Let him see the cloud formations, the sunset, the early morning, the big dipper, the little dipper, the milky way, and the evening star. Let him hear the birds sing. Constantly call his attention to

these things, reminding him Who is behind it all.

At the end of each day ask the child what he has seen today that is beautiful and that was made by God. Make this a little ritual. See to it that the little child's mind is fixed upon God regularly at the same time every day. See that he interweaves the day's activities with the workings of God. This will create habits that will be with him all of his life.

There was a day in America when we were a rural society. This is no longer true. Our society has become urbanized to the extent that we are so prone to miss the blessings of beholding the beauties around us, of hearing God's great harmonies, and of feeling the breath of God. Most adults are so busy grasping for success that we have arrived at our destination but have missed the beauties beside the road as we traveled. Hence, we have become successful but have not learned how to enjoy its benefits. This would not be true if someone had disciplined us to revere God when we were little ones.

5. *Indelibly imprint in the mind of the little child that the Bible is the Word of God and that Jesus is the Son of God*. When I was a little boy my mother used to hold the Bible before me and say, "Son, the Bible is the Word of God. Say it, son." I would repeat, "The Bible is the Word of God." Again and again this was repeated. Then my mother would say, "Son, the Bible is about Jesus. Jesus is the Son of God. Say it, son." I would then reply, "Jesus is the Son of God." Then she would ask me to say it again and again and again and again until it was indelibly imprinted in my mind: the Bible is the Word of God and Jesus is the Son of God!

When Becky (my oldest daughter) was newborn and still in the maternity ward at the hospital I brought a big Bible and held it up before the window. I shouted through the window, "Becky, this is the

Word of God," and I waved the Bible from side to side. (I am not sure that she was impressed!)

The first day she was home from the hospital I put. her on the floor, got the Bible, and told her how to be saved. I did this every week even when she was an infant. I am not sure when the moment was that salvation's plan first dawned upon her, but I am sure that she knew how to be saved, for regularly I took the Bible, went to her crib, and told her about Adam and Eve, the depravity of man, the wrath of God, God's plan of salvation, the atonement, the resurrection, etc. I wanted to be sure she associated her daddy with a black book called the Bible and in her subconscious mind was registered God's plan of salvation. How important this is in the life of a child.

Charles Darwin with his theory of evolution has turned many young lives away from the Bible and God. It is said that when he was a young man he was a great lover of poetry, but because of his desire for scientific achievement did not develop this side of his nature. Later when he had time to enjoy poetry he found he could not enjoy it, for he had not developed this particular appetite and it had died from inactivity. It is so important that our children not only be taught reverence, but they must be taught to have reverence and to offer reverence and adoration to God even before they are old enough to know how to be saved.

6. *When the little child has done wrong, explain to him that the punishment you are giving is given from God and that you are acting as God's representative in meting out the punishment.* Let Him know that it is not the parent who sets right and wrong or determines what is sin; it is God Who does that. Let the child know that it is not the parent's idea to punish but that he has been instructed by God to punish. On the other hand, let the child know that

the good things which happen to him and are done
for him and given to him by the parent are actually
gifts from God. In other words, that which the parent
does for and to the child which is Scriptural should
be explained to the child. He should know that the
things we do to and for him which are Scriptural are
things we do at God's command. This will make God
part of our every day conversation and the child will
grow up not feeling ill at ease when he talks about
God.

7. *The child should be taught to respect the man
of God and revere his office.* A little girl once drew a
picture. Her father asked her what the picture was.
She replied, "It is a picture of God." The father
chuckled and said, "Well, sweetheart, no one knows
what God looks like." "They do now," the child
replied.

Once I tied a little boy's shoe. He looked up at his
mother, who was a very poor lady, and with a tear in
his eye and excitement in his voice he said, "Mother,
did you see God tie my shoe?"

There was a little boy in my church who called me
"Brother God." When I would be preaching some
Sunday morning on hell fire and damnation he would
look up at his mother and say, "Mama, ain't God mad
today!"

One day when I was talking to my son, David,
when he was a little fellow I asked him what he had
learned in Sunday school. He said he had learned
about God. "What else?" I asked.

"I learned that God loves me more than anybody
loves me," he replied.

"What else did you learn?"

"I learned that God spanks me when I do wrong."
"What else?"

"I learned then that God loves me and tells me it
hurt Him worse than it did . . . Hey, Dad, are you

God?"

One of the fine families in our church recently had a baby. When the mother arrived home from the hospital with the little boy, Timothy, one of the older children took a look at him and exclaimed, "Mother, Timothy will have to get a haircut or Brother Hyles won't let him in the nursery!" You see, the child's hairline was rather low and he had so much hair that he looked as if he needed a haircut, and the older children knew my stand on long hair.

One of the precious little girls in our church recently wrote me a note. It was my birthday and she said, "Happy Birthday. I am so grateful for a great and wonderful preacher. You don't know how grateful I am to you for doing so much for me...I used to be a flop in school, but I am at a Christian school and it's because you have done this for me. I don't know how much I do love you, but I love you so much that I can't even write it. I love you very, much. Love in Christ, (signed)."

Some parents have been on the job, haven't they? They have been teaching their children to respect the pastor. If children respect the man of God, they will respect the God Whom the man represents when they get old enough to know Him. However, in early childhood, it is hard for a child to disassociate God from a person.

A little girl asked her mother for something. The mother replied, "Sweetheart, ask God for it." The little girl again asked her mother. Again the mother said, "I told you to ask God for it!" The little girl whimpered, "But Mother, I want to ask someone who's got skin on him." Children need to see God in us and His love exemplified in us.

One little child in our church said to her mother, "God is watching over us all the time. He dosen't even take a coffee break."

Dr. Walt Handford, who pastors a church, has a son who was once watching television on a Saturday. The child heard the announcer say, "Don't forget, boys and girls, tomorrow is Sunday. Go to the church of your choice." The little fellow looked at his mother and said, "Mother, we can't do that, can we?"

Dr. John Rice has a grandson who went to health class at school and came home and told his parents, "Today we learned all about mouth-to-mouth recreation!"

Yes, children are impressionable and if they can be taught reverence for God, it will be much easier for them to accept God's Christ when they understand that He died for them.

Of course, reverence should be created with a constant emphasis on high ideals and morals and with the proper example from the mother and father.

Chapter Five

HOW TO FORM THE PROPER HABITS IN A CHILD

Habits make character. If one forms good habits, he will have good character. If he forms bad habits, he will have bad character. The word "character" comes from a word which mean "to cut" or "to engrave." Each time an act is performed a deeper groove is made until one has done a certain thing so often in a particular way that it is difficult to change. H. W. Shaw said, "It is easy to assume a habit; but when you try to cast it off, it will take skin and all." The more that one has the same emotion or action the more it deepens the track and the easier it is to be repeated. This is true when a child is taught to eat, to button his clothes, to tie his shoes, to dress himself, etc. At first he has to think to do it. He does the same thing until it is done without his will or thoughts. He can now tie his shoes and never think what he is doing. He can walk with a thousand other things on his mind. He can dress himself without thinking. He has developed a habit. The action has been indelibly impressed on the nervous system. The parent who wants his child to grow up to be a good, strong person will be disappointed if he does not form the right habits in him. These habits must be formed by repetition until he does things entirely automatically with no thought or will behind his actions. Hence, his tasks are not performed by present effort but by past preparation.

Once a war veteran was carrying a sack of potatoes when suddenly someone who wanted to pull a joke on him shouted, "Attention!" Instinctively the ex - soldier brought his hands to his side and the potatoes fell in the street.

I once knew a soldier who was left-handed. The first day he was in the army he saluted an officer. Instinctively he did it with his left hand. After much practice he was able to salute with his right hand throughout his military days. He himself became an officer. The day he was to get his discharge he was so happy. On his way to the separation center to receive his discharge papers he was saluted by a private. Instinctively he saluted back with his left hand! He was still left-handed and no amount of adult training could change his childhood habits.

The more we live by doing right automatically and the more our good habits save us the making of excessive choices, the better we will be and the more we will do. Precarious is the life of a person whose daily actions have not become habitual and who must exercise his will every time he does something. He will become tired in his work, more laborious in his deliberations, and less efficient in all he does. Those who have to use their wills for every momentary matter of business without the help of habit are not as efficient as those who have learned to become disciplined enough to make their actions mechanical. Someone has said that habit is a labor-saving device that causes the disciplined person to get along with less fuel. The wise personnel officer checks concerning his applicant's habits; those of honesty, gambling, etc. Proper habits can write a check that is always redeemable.

Samuel Johnson wrote, "The change of habits is in general too small to be felt until they are too strong to be broken." It is said that on Plato's ring there was a motto written, "It is easier to prevent ill habits than to break them."

History is filled with the names of great men whose accomplishments were aided by their mental ability. This hall of heroes would include Einstein, Edison, and many others. Yet, along side these names would be the names of others who did not become men of renown because of their mental genius but because of their character and their loyalty to habit. Such men as Livingston, Franklin, Lincoln, Luther, and others teach us that a man of character with average intelligence can do the work of a genius. This is true because character seeks talent. The proper character seeks out the talent necessary to perform a job, whereas talent often flees from character. Talent often does not recognize its need for character. Character always recognizes it need for talent.

The argument for character and habit having been presented, we now advance the following suggestions as ways and means of creating proper habits in the life of a child.

1. *Have the child perform the same proper thing over and over again.* The action should be performed frequently and continuously. No opportunity to do it should be missed and no break should be made in its regularity. No omission should be allowed. The tendency to act spontaneously can become ingrained in a child only in direct proportion to the uninterrupted frequency which the child does the act. Do it; do it again; do it again and again and again. Keep doing it. Do it regularly. Epictetus said, "If you would make a thing a habit, do it." Horace Mann said, "Habit is a cable; we weave a thread of it each day and it becomes so strong we cannot break it."

2. *Teach the child to do regularly now what he wants to do later habitually.* Never let him be guilty of such statements as, "When I get to be a man I am going to do thus and so." Unless the habits of

diligence, punctuality, etc. are formed as a boy, there will be no great accomplishments that come suddenly as a man.

One day a father returned from a bear hunt. His young boy said, "I'll be glad when I get to be a man so I can hunt some bears," whereupon his father replied, "Son, there are some little bears in the forest too!" I have watched young people for years. I have seen ministerial students who prepared themselves in college to do something later, but they did nothing in college. I have seen other students who formed the proper habits of work, study, etc. in college. They continued using these habits in their lives and success became inevitable. Teach the child, "Do it now! Do it now!" One who is not courageous as a boy will not suddenly do courageous acts as a man.

3. *Help the child build a schedule.* Disciplined people live by schedule. I am writing this chapter in my hotel room in Green Lake, Wisconsin. In the lobby of this hotel there are dozens of Christian workers sitting around talking. I have scheduled my day so as to spend some time writing these truths. Because of that I cannot enjoy the extravagance of what they call "fellowship." If I am successful and get my work done, I must follow my schedule with strict discipline.

Take the child out in the snow. Have him walk over the snow one time. Then tell him to retrace his steps. Now it is easier to walk, for he is taking the same path. Have him continue to follow the same path over and over again. Notice how a regular path is formed because the particles have been pressed down. Soon he will take the path unconsciously because he has trodden it so many times. Due to this fact the path is easier to tread. The same is true with habit. It is acquired when one disciplines himself by schedule. Train the child at an early age to do so. He should get up at the same time every morning. He should go to bed at the same time each evening. He should eat his meals as near the same time each day as possible. He should brush his teeth at the same time and the same place. He should bathe at the same time daily. Even if his body is not dirty enough to demand a bath, habit is certainly a worthy reason for regular bathing. Maybe he could have a regular night to wash his hair, etc. Routine and schedule are vital aids in the building of habit which is necessary in the building of character.

4. *The parent must be the example for the child.* He must be what he wishes the child to become. Hence, the child will see a living visual aid of what he should become. The parent must not fail to be prompt. regular, responsible, truthful, etc. He must be the embodiment of the truths that he teaches.

5. *Make the child do what he does not especially like to do.* Suppose a girl does not like doing the dishes. The mother should then force the girl to do them regularly until doing the dishes becomes habit, routine, and perhaps even enjoyable. Find the habits that each child does not enjoy and does not do regularly. See that they are done by schedule and promptly. Nothing that is right to do should ever become distasteful to the child. It should be repeated over and over again. If it is a distasteful chore, it can become habitual. Hence, it will be done because the will is not brought into action each time the act is performed.

6. *Teach the child that if he wants to avoid bad habits, he should not do something bad even the first time.* If something is not done for the first time, it will not become a habit. He who does not tell the first lie will not become a liar. He who does not steal the first thing will not become a thief. He who does not drink his first drink will not become an alcoholic.

He that never utters a profane word will not become a profane person. There can be no habit until there is a second.

Take the child to the top of a steep slide. Have him get on a sled. Tell him to decide halfway down the hill that he wants to return and see what success he has. The place to decide is before he takes the first step.

Young people like to say, "I know when to stop." This may be true. A person can know WHEN to stop but habit will not let him stop. That which one does not want to make habitual should not be done the first time!

7. *It is good for a child to admit publicly a decision to do right and to quit doing wrong*. This is why it is wise in churches for a child to walk the aisle during the invitation and declare to the pastor a decision he is making. It is often wise for the pastor to make public that decision so as to commit the child publicly. The wise parent will suggest that his child walk the aisle when he makes his spiritual decisions declaring to someone else what he intends to do. This will make it harder for him to change his mind, and better still, to change his actions.

8. *See that the children associate with people with habit*. Encourage them to be around orderly people when they are very little. See to it that family friends are people of order, discipline, and character. Make heroes of such people in the mind of the child. Soon he will emulate the right kind of people.

9. *Have some family rituals that will necessitate schedule and discipline, thereby teaching the child routine and habit*. When the children are very young there may be a certain night of the week when certain things are done. Perhaps one night could be eating - out night, one night could be game night, one night could be midnight snack night, etc. The more things

that can be done at the same time each day or each week the more the child's schedule will govern his life. The more habit can prevent the overexercising of his will, the more he will avoid the making of an excessive number of decisions, for these decisions are made by reflex, by schedule, by discipline, by routine, etc.

10. *There should be regularity and order at home.* There should be a time and place for everything. Towels should always be kept on the same shelf. The dishes should always be at the same place. Meals should be served at the same time, and in general, there should be an order, a proper arrangement, and regularity about the activities and events at home.

This is one reason why I travel across the country encouraging preachers to do things properly in their churches. A church that starts on time, presents only those musical numbers that are properly planned and presented, and in general does things always decently and in order, will teach a perennial lesson to its young people and children: that God's work should be done in the best way possible and that no slothfulness or haphazard performances should be associated with the Lord's work. With the home, church, and school working together as examples of order and regularity, the child will be reared in an atmosphere of discipline and proper habit. Consequently, he will have a greater opportunity to develop good character. If he sees smiles, he will smile more himself. If he sees the parent being frugal and punctual, the pastor exemplifying intergrity and discipline, and the teacher being an example of regularity and order, he himself will soon reflect his environment and those who create it.

11. *The parent should always attach the result with the act.* The words "drink" and "drunkard" should be associated. The words "dope" and "addict"

should be associated. The words "lazy" and "poverty" should be associated. Psychologically the child should be trained to associate the end with the act. In other words, the child should always know to what the act will lead. Show him some people who are at the end of the road he wants to travel. Let him see alcoholics and remind him that they once took their "first" drink. Take him to skid row and show him the end of the first step. Take him to a neighborhood where poverty prevails and show him where laziness often ends. Fix in his mind always the distasteful end of a presently tasteful wrong.

How many time have wrongdoers said, "I did not think!" This is so true. "Rightdoers" can also say the same thing. When a person has to think to do right, he has not developed the proper character. If by habit he does right, he can truthfully say, "I did not think." The person who develops the wrong habits can truthfully say, "I simply did not think before I did it." If he had had the proper rearing and training, he would not have had to think first. The groove would have been so deep because of the habitual performance of right that he would not have done wrong. Remember, character is habit! Habit is formed by the proper and continuous repetition of doing right.

Chapter Six

WORK

"Go to the ant, thou sluggard; consider her ways, and be wise: Which having no guide, overseer, or ruler, Provideth her meat in the summer, and gathereth her food in the harvest. How long wilt thou sleep, O sluggard? when wilt thou arise out of thy sleep? Yet a little sleep, a little slumber, a little folding of the hands to sleep: So shall thy poverty come as one that travelleth, and thy want as an armed man." (Proverbs 6:6-11)

No parent can be successful in rearing a child unless he teaches the child to work hard. No child can develop character without developing a willingness to work and an affinity for work. God did for man a great favor when He told him he would earn his bread by the sweat of his brow. The old proverb says, "An idle mind is the devil's workshop." Someone has said, "Idleness is the mother of sin." So really when God commanded man to work He was commanding him to be moral and to have a right outlet for nerve force which if not used, would find vent in wrong outlets. Hence, God uses labor to train us in obedience, self-control, perseverance, etc. Work is a tool which God uses to make men. In order to make men and women of character out of our boys and girls, we must teach them to work.

1. *Teach them very early to help in the home.* In the earliest years of a child's life he has a natural instinct to help. Girls like to "play house" and dust, scrub, wash, sweep, make doll dresses, etc. Boys like

51

to "play store" and make things. It is then that the child wants to help, and work is play to him. The wise parent will be careful not to destroy this instinct. During these early formative years the child should be taught that work is not a burden. It is not an evil, but rather something in which he can delight.

Do not associate in the child's mind that work is drudgery. Seize upon the natural instinct that God has given a little child by teaching him that work is proper, normal, and yes, even delightful.

2. *Encourage the child to make his own toys.* It seems to me unwise to buy too many toys. Perhaps it would be better to buy the child the tools enabling him to make his own toys. The parent could join the child as he makes his toys and perhaps even things for the home. Hence, the child will be far ahead of the other children. He has been trained to realize that if he buys it, he forfeits the fun of making it. Even the tiniest of toys I ever had, I made myself. I can recall making carts, cars, scooters that had skates for wheels, slingshots, sleds, kites, etc. Girls could make doll clothes, doll house furnishings, etc. Not only doest this teach the children initiative, but it also makes them thrifty.

3. *Children should help in household tasks.* At a very early age children should be taught to clean their rooms and make their beds. It should be their regular duty and if the performance is less than acceptable, the parent should not correct it, but should point out to the child the weaknesses, thus teaching him to finish the job he has started. There are many chores that even a little child can do around the house such as making the beds, wiping the dishes, cleaning the room, emptying the garbage cans, taking care of pets, setting the table, etc. Regular duties should be given the child when he is old enough to begin.

4. *The child should be taught that he is a part of a*

team and that he is slack at his job if he does not work.
He should think of himself as an integral part
of society, a part that is essential to the whole. He
must feel each of us must work to do some service for
the rest of us and that if one person does not do his
work, he is not being fair to others. It is like one
player on a team not doing his best. An old proverb
says, "An idle man is of no more use than a dead man
and takes up more room." It is not right or fair as
members of this great team of labor.

5. *Teach the child to do his best at whatever he
does.* When he does his best brag on him and magnify
his efforts. When he doesn't do his best let your
disappointment be shown. Of course, this is only
workable when the parent has built a close
relationship with the child so that the child's heart
will be broken when he displeases the parent. We are
admonished in the Scriptures to do everything that
we do with all our might. Someone has said, "He who
is afraid of doing too much always does too little." By
constant reminder and praise the wise parent
impresses indelibly in the mind of the child that
anything that is worth doing is worth doing right. The
job should always be done a little bit better than
when someone else does it.

It has been said that there are three classes of
people: those who fail to do all their duty, those who
do all of their duty, and those who do a little more
than their duty. The first lose their positions; the
second hold them; and the third are promoted.

6. *The child should not be allowed to think that
labor which is done with the hands is dirty work.*
Parents should make all work honorable and insist on
honest, hard work. No matter what the work is, if it
is honest and well done, it is dignified and honorable.
Let him know that every job has its own particular
charms and interests, and the more he knows about

the job the more interesting it becomes. Hence, whatever one does, if he does it well, he should feel a sense of pride and accomplishment.

When I was a young man working my way through college, for eighteen months I laid oak floor for a living. For several months I put up dry wall. I have been a salesman, and I have worked in a service station and in a grocery store. Once I was a paper boy. In the Army I was a paratrooper and a parachute packer. I have worked in mechanics shops, loaded box cars, sold in clothing stores, and once in the Army I was on the garbage collecting gang. In every job I felt a unique pride if I worked and did my best. I even found a new way to stack garbage in the truck and became the envy of all the garbage collectors.

The child should not be afraid of perspiration or hard work. Whatever his job, if it is a proper one and if it helps society, it should develop a sense of pride. Of course, if this attitude is developed, it is because the parent stresses it to the child.

This means that one should prepare himself properly for any task and give himself to it completely. The more he knows about the job the more interesting it will become.

7.   *The child should be encouraged to have constructive hobbies.* Even leisure can be work, and work can be rest. Rest is simply the changing from the use of one set of nerves and muscles to another. The postman rests in an air-conditioned room; the executive rests by taking a walk or hike. City folk rest by going to the country for the weekend; country folk rest by going to the city for the weekend. George Bernard Shaw once said, "Happy is the man that makes his living at his hobby." A famous baseball star said that he was happy because he was getting paid for what he preferred to do.

If the child can be taught to use his spare time

constructively, he is a few steps ahead of the others. The making of model airplanes and handcraft can help the child prepare for either a vocation or an avocation. Hence, he is taught to enjoy work rather than leisure and that part of his life which is not given to his vocation can be a constructive part. Many of the greatest works ever written were written by men who were employed in fields other than writing, but who used their leisure for writing. Marcus Aurelius wrote his meditations in moments of rest.

8. *Teach a child to choose an occupation that helps mankind.* There are many jobs that are of no service to one's fellow human beings. Children should be taught to respect the work of the carpenter, doctor, preacher, farmer, garbage collector, baker, merchant, lawyer, etc. A vocation should not be chosen because it is one's preference or solely because one enjoys doing it. High on the list of criteria should be its service to fellowman and its making of a part of this aforementioned team of society. No occupation should be just a means to make a living but rather a means of service to others.

For years I have encouraged my young people to play sports as a hobby but not to consider professional sports. They should enjoy music but not consider a professional career in music. Of course, no one should enter a profession that caters to the lower instincts and hinders society. Such professions as working in a factory that produces liquor or tobacco and being a bartender, a barmaid, etc. should be taboo. Every vocation should be one of service and one that helps our fellowmen. One of the finest statements in the Bible is said of David when it was said of him that he "served his own generation by the will of God." (Acts 13:36)

Once there was a man who inherited a good name and much money. He did not participate in the life of his community; he dedicated his life to riotous living. He went through the money, spent it on pleasure, and died leaving his money to another. However, a small portion of his money was left to a publisher with instructions to the publisher to prepare and issue his biography. When the book was finished it was beautiful and costly. The binding was elaborate. There was a title page and picture of the deceased. Then on page one was recorded the day of his birth. On the last page of the book was recorded the date of his death. The rest of the book was simply expensive blank paper. The biographer was saying that this man was born and died and in between did nothing for others. How sad! It is sadder, however, to realize how few parents instill in the minds of their children the importance of choosing a profession that will benefit society.

9.   *Stress should be given that one should work hard even without an overseer.* Teach the child that someone is always watching. Tell him about that great cloud of heavenly witnesses in Hebrews 12:1. While he is very young lead him to realize that those in the family that have gone on to Heaven are watching. Many years ago when I was a little boy my mother called me off to the side and said, "Son, I want to tell you something. You have three sisters: one that you can see and two whom you cannot see but who can see you. They are in Heaven. Each went when she was seven. Remember, son, that they are always watching you, so live your life to make them proud." This is one of the incentives God has used to make me work hard through the years.

This chapter is being dictated on an airplane. I am flying to Los Angeles, California, where I shall speak for a few days. The lady across the aisle from me is reading a book; the couple sitting next to me are drinking champagne; four people behind me are playing cards; the man in front of me is sound asleep; the fellow behind me is reading a magazine; I can see no one who is working! Far too many of us work only if we are watched. The parent who teaches his child that someone is always watching and that he should work without an overseer is doing him a great favor. One personnel man said, "For every two men that I employ, I have to employ a third to oversee them." Employers are eagerly searching for people who will work without oversight. Such people go to the top. The fellow who cannot do so, stays at the foot, has the same job, draws the same salary, hates his work, and grows old too soon!

10. *Do not ascribe success to genius.* A genius comes along only occasionally. Most of us are just common, average people with common, average minds. Hence, the difference between success and failure is not genius, it is hard work! This means working while others sleep, toiling while others play, and planning while others idle away their time.

I know many great men. Few of them have brilliant minds but all are hard workers who use all the ability they possess. By all means, stress to the child that success is caused not by genius or by being a mental giant, but rather, by hard work, diligence, discipline, etc.

11. *Make no provisions for failure.* This has been a motto of my life. Such statements as "What should I do if I fail?" should not even be tolerated. If provision is made for failure, then thought must be given to failure. If thought is given to failure, then one has considered the possibility of failing. Such possibilities should never be considered. There is too much stress on being a "good loser." Now to be sure when losses do come, outwardly we should accept them gracefully, but inwardly we should despise defeat! No child should be taught to accept defeat gracefully inwardly. He should

hate defeat. He should make no provision for failure and should be surprised if it comes.

Many of us brag on our child more if he loses gracefully than if he wins. We are in some sense guilty of raising a generation of people who like to lose. We need to build a generation of people with a passion to win!

If one plans to win, he will make no provision for failure.

12. *No child should have to bear the burden of having a lot of money left to him.* James Fargo, as President of the American Express Company, once said, "If I were worth a hundred million, I would make my son earn his living. It is wrong to bring up boys to be gentlemen loafers." Rather than leaving children a lot of money, why not leave them what will make them money and give them the privilege of earning it themselves!

I was once talking to the son of a famous preacher. Suddenly I looked him in the eye and said, "I feel sorry for you."

He asked, "Why?"

I then replied, "I feel sorry for you because your father is so famous."

He began to weep and said, "Dr. Hyles, I didn't know anybody ever thought of that. I envy you because your father was a drunkard. Nobody expected you to be successful. Everybody expected me to be so."

This condition was unavoidable, but it is possible for one to avoid the leaving of great sums of money to his children. He does them a disservice, not a service!

13. *The child should be taught to work cheerfully.* His parents should set the example of enjoying their work. It is actually possible for one to look forward to a "day on" and not to a "day off."

This is the way it ought to be. To say the least, a day at work should not be considered worse than a day at home, and a day of toil should not be considered worse than a day of rest. Each is a diversion from the other. Hence, work should be approached and done cheerfully, happily, and enthusiastically. This will take away the despair that often comes when one has to work on what is otherwise a day off. It will remove grumbling when overtime is necessary, and it will certainly equip the child with the tools that can take him to the top.

14. *Teach him that all work is an art and a way of expression.* Hence, one should look upon himself as an artist regardless of what type of work he does. When a bricklayer becomes an artist he becomes a builder. When a typist becomes an artist she becomes a secretary. When a meat cutter becomes an artist, he becomes a butcher. When the carpenter becomes an artist, he becomes a builder. When a cook becomes an artist, he becomes a chef. When a speaker becomes an artist, he becomes an orator. When a bookkeeper becomes an artist, he is an accountant. When a plumber becomes an artist, he is a pipefitter. When a custodian becomes an artist, he is a maintenance engineer. No work, no matter how slight or insignificant, should be despised. Whether one is sweeping out the place, mending socks, mowing yards, or shoveling snow, he should be an artist about it. It is somewhat sad that in our day the assembly line at the factory has eliminated such pride in one's work, but even with the assembly line the wise worker will develop pride and consider his work an art.

When I was attending a state university as a young man I simply had to find part-time work. No jobs were available, so I began laying oak floor. What a job! What a backbreaker! The first few days were sheer drudgery. Then I resolved to become the best oak floor layer in the county. I began thinking about the families that would live in the houses I helped to build. When each house was completed I would drive by it again and again and take pleasure in the realization that someone was enjoying the fruit of my work. I looked upon myself as an artist and soon I began taking pride in the opportunity of telling others my vocation. It has been about a quarter of a century since I have laid a piece of oak floor, but I still enjoy going back to the old home neighborhood and driving by the houses that I helped to build.

15. *A child should be taught that hard work is healthy.* No one can reach his peak of physical health unless he has learned to work. Work is nature's medicine. Just as idlenesss rusts and decays a machine so the disuse of a muscle causes it to shrivel. The doctors find agreement in the fact that many men and women are in sanatoriums because of a lack of good, hard, steady work. In such places patients are put to work immediately. Especially is this true in cases of those that suffer from nervous disorders. Without work the body becomes weak and the brain deteriorates. A girl should be taught that work is a beauty aid and the boy should be taught that work is a body-building device. Parents should point to heroes and remind the children that they obtained their positions through hard work.

16. *Young people should be taught trades.* A poll was taken in one penitentiary which revealed that 90% of the convicts answered "no trade" on a questionnaire. In a certain period there were 3,154 boys admitted. Not one of them had a trade. Consequently, all of them were taught trades and only 14% of them returned!

During the period that a young person is usually taught a trade he is also facing his greatest temptations. Hence, the learning of the trade keeps him busy at a time when his mind is most susceptible to temptation.

In some ancient societies it was a law that no man was under obligation to support his father when his father became aged if his parents had not taught him a trade in his youth. Perhaps this is a little severe but it does not alter the fact that the wise father will teach his son a trade, and the wise mother will carefully and deliberately teach her daughter to prepare for marriage and motherhood with the same diligence that a physician prepares for his vocation.

17. *Always compliment the task that is finished and done well.* The reward method is an important one to a child. He should always associate completion with rewards. To the contrary he should always associate failure and an unfinished task with disappointment on the face of one he loves.

18. *The child should be taught to accomplish the hardest and most distasteful part of the task first.*
Perhaps he should eat first the vegetable he likes least. Perhaps he should mow the hardest part of the yard first. This helps to prevent the awful sin of procrastination.

There are many other things that parents should teach their children concerning the proper development of work habits such as teaching them to choose their heroes from ones who have worked their way from the bottom to the top, teaching them to choose a profession that will enable them to leave something for others when they are gone, teaching them to be thrifty and yet generous with money earned, etc., but in it all there should shine forth an ability to work and the dignity of labor.

Chapter Seven

TEACHING INDEPENDENCE AND
SELF-RELIANCE

Our world today is crying for leadership, for someone whom the crowd will follow. Such a one must not follow the crowd. He must learn to stand on his own feet, to be his own man, and to be self-reliant. Hence, the child must be taught to think for himself and believe in himself. A planned course of action should be plotted by every parent to train his child so he will not feel he is dependent on society, but rather can make his own way, holding his head high and being his own man. In order to achieve this goal there are certain ingredients which are vital.

Someone has said that men are cast iron while children are clay. Hence, the subject matter covered in this chapter is not for the adult to attach awkwardly to his molded character, but rather for the child to learn and do while his character is being molded.

1. *Encourage him to solve his own problems as often as possible.* Encourage him to express his own ideas.

2. *Lead the child to think always, "Is there any way to improve upon this?"* This does not mean that he imposes his will outside his own sphere of occupation. It does mean, however, that in his own mind he should think over and over again about as many matters as possible, "Can I think of any way to improve on this?" Even if he is not asked and does not have the opportunity to put into action these thoughts, he is nevertheless preparing himself for improvements when the opportunity is presented.

Along these same lines teach him to think of a solution to all problems. A person who wants to help others will be ready to help when the opportunity presents itself. This does not mean he should be bothersome and enter into an area where he is not welcome or needed. It does mean, however, that he should be ready to help if he is asked to help. Consequently, the more problems that one can find solutions to the more available he will be when his help is needed or asked.

Gospel singer Bill Harvey after having observed this author for many years said one time, "Dr. Hyles, I would suggest you never to go to Italy." When asked the reason he replied, "Because you would try to straighten the leaning tower of Pisa."

God will always provide the opportunity in His own time for a prepared man.

3.   *Teach the child initiative.* Initiative is simply the doing of something without being told. If there is a job to be done, the child does it. It also implies self-confidence and self-reliance. Emerson said, "Trust thyself." Initiative teaches one to do this.

4.   *Whenever possible give the child a choice between two or three courses of action.* In other words, say to him, "Here are three choices. You cannot do them all, but you must do one." Let the child choose. The parent should say, "Johnny, you may have either this one or that one. You may go either this way or that way." (Be sure that both choices are morally right.) "You may wear this garment or that garment. You may eat this food or that food." In other words, the parent should find some choices either of which is acceptable to him. Let the child make a choice thereby getting him into the habit of making decisions on his own. Once the choice is made, be sure the child is held firmly to his decision. He is being taught to be a person of

decision. Note carefully he is not being taught to choose between right and wrong. He is being taught to choose the most beneficial right. Again, remember, do not allow him to waver after he has made his choice. Someone once asked Alexander what was the cause of his success. He answered, "By not wavering." Someone has said, "Deliberate with caution and then act with decision."

5. *Teach the child to make a quick decision once he has thought it over carefully.* This is not to say that the child should make a decision without properly weighing the facts. He should be quick to make a firm decision after all the facts have been gathered and weighed.

To aid in the development of such decision making, the parent could present a problem to a child. This problem has to do with making a decision. Give him a set period of time to think about it and insist upon the decision by that time. For example, the parent could tell the child that he has five minutes to make up his mind. The next time the same problem is presented give him four minutes, then three, etc.

There are times in the life of every child when he must make a quick decision. Much will rest upon this. He should be trained to act almost by reflex, and he can if he has been properly prepared.

At this point the reader may want to indict the author if he does not stop to realize that the author is not advocating rash and hasty decisions. He is simply desirous of combating extensive thinking and indecision when nothing can be accomplished. One should do his best and then be satisfied. If he has made a mistake, he has learned the knowledge that will help him next time. One should not waste time in regret but face the next decision. Certainly one should not undo in doubt what he has done in faith!

6. *Do not oversympathize with the child.* This teaches him to whine and seek sympathy. If he is going to be his own man, he must learn to face hardships, stand alone, and be willing to suffer without a martyr's complex.

My son, David, at this writing plays on the high school basketball team. Last year he was injured in a game and carried off the floor writhing in pain. I was sitting about 25 feet from him and of course, I was very apprehensive and concerned. However, instead of rushing to his side, I let him be alone for awhile. When the attention was taken off of him I slipped over quietly and said, "How is it, doc?"

With a pained expression on his face he said, "I'm okay, Dad, go ahead."

As I walked away I said, "He is becoming a man."

One of the great mistakes made in rearing children is overprotection and oversympathy. People who have no obstacles to overcome and face no hardships are usually weak-willed. Just as muscles are made stronger by use the will is made stronger by use. Hence, early in the life of a child we must see to it that people do not carry on over him with excessive sympathy. To some parents this will seem hard-boiled and harsh. What they do not realize is that they are the ones who are hard-boiled and harsh, for they are training a child by habit to whine. Someday he will be unable to face his hardships alone. Hence, he will cast himself on society and become a liability rather than an asset.

Someone has said that a piece of iron in its rough state is worth about $5. After being made into a horse shoe it is worth about $12. When made into knife blades it is worth $1000. When made into balance springs for watches it is worth $250,000. What is the difference? The difference is that as this iron goes through certain processes and is heated, hammered, rolled, pressed, cut, polished, beaten, formed, etc., it is becoming more useful. The same is true with a child.

One of the great reasons for juvenile deliquency and youth socialistic groups, etc. is that the children are born with the proverbial silver spoon in their mouths. They never face hardship, never have to work hard, and consequently, are reared thinking they are owed a living. Even young eagles must fly, for the old eagles turn them out as soon as they are able to fly.

7. *The child should be taught to make his own way.* This does not take an extraordinary brain. School teachers often tell me that the most brilliant pupils often disappoint them. This is because they can do things easily. They do not have to learn to concentrate or to be diligent. They have to face no hardships. Hence, the child with mediocre ability reaches his goal with grit and determination. Because of this he develops the processes that make for greatness. Mental brilliance does not make for greatness. Perseverance, work, character, diligence, industry, and thrift are the causes that make one great. When these qualities have to be developed one can become great without mental brilliance, whereas the mentally brilliant will usually not develop these qualities.

8. *When the child reaches the age of six or seven let him earn some money and spend it on his own.* Perhaps he can work in the yard for an hour and make a quarter. Then send him by himself down to the corner store to spend it alone. He will learn two things: He will learn to be careful about spending his money, for he had to work an hour to get it. He will also learn to make decisions and to go somewhere on his own. If the store is several miles away, the wise parent will drive the child to within a block of the

store, let him out, let him go alone to make his purchase and return to the car. He is learning that necessary fact of life that he must someday be on his own. He is being prepared for that day.

9. *As soon as possible let him have his own bicycle and go places alone.* Bear in mind we are trying to teach the child independence and self-reliance. Far too many parents put the child in the family car and take him anywhere he wants to go. How sad! Mom becomes a taxi driver for some spoiled, lazy children, and the Dad who does not want his son to go through the hardships he endured has taken from his son the very qualitites that made him successful. The wise dad will want his son to endure some hardships, for hardships endured early will prevent greater hardships to be endured later, for the child will have learned to face life.

10. *Give him some responsibilities of his own.* As soon as possible throw him upon his own resources by giving him responsibilities. Give him a task to perform. Make him perform it to its completion. Do not correct it or finish it for him. He must realize that it is his task and that he must do it. He must know that if he does not do it, it will not be done!

I am grateful that at the age of ten I had my first paper route. I became a businessman. I had responsibility and obligation. I had to face it. There were decisions I had to make and no one could make them for me. I have thanked God many times for this opportunity.

11. *Teach the child to repair things that are broken.* Give to the boy the responsibility of being the repairman around the house. Let him tinker and learn how to fix things. Let the girl mend and sew. Along the same line do not purchase for a child what he can make for himself. In another chapter we discussed the fact that a child should make his own

toys if at all possible. When we were boys we made such things as scooters, go-carts, slingshots, etc. This is vital in the proper emotional development of a child.

12. *Teach a boy to defend himself.* The manly art of self-defense should be a part of every boy's development. Teach him to box. Teach him to shoot. Teach him self-defense. A man should have the idea that he can take care of himself, that he can protect those who are his own, and that he can be in charge of the situation. To some this sounds cocky. In a socialistic world it may be that confidence is mistaken for arrogance by those who are not self-reliant.

When my boy was five years of age I bought him a pair of boxing gloves; in fact, I bought two pairs— one for the boy across the street and one for my boy. They squared off in the basement and I taught my son how to defend himself. Now he can protect his sisters and he has done so. He also has the feeling that he can take care of himself. This is important for self-reliance.

13. *A child should be taught to do one thing and do it well.* He should have one aim, one direction. Point his energies in one pursuit. He should know where he is going and learn how to get there. He should direct his activities toward that one goal. It is tragic to see middle-aged men still trying to decide what they are going to be and do in their lives. Such often become professional students who later bounce from one job to another and are always going to be something great "tomorrow."

A little boy was shooting a B-B gun up in the air when a man passing by asked him at what he was shooting. He replied, "The moon."

The man laughed and said, "Why, you can't hit the moon with a B-B gun!"

"No," said the boy, "but I'm a lot closer than you are." Goals are so important!

14. *The child should be taught to look out for the needs of others.* He should not think of his own desires, but the desires and needs of other people. The parent should point to those in need and teach the child compassion. He should instruct the child to do what he can to alleviate the suffering and satisfy the needs of society.

The other day I was visiting my mother. She will soon be 84. She asked about the children and then we started talking about Dave. She informed me that he makes a habit of seeing her at church and chatting with her for awhile. He also is not ashamed to place a kiss upon her brow. Then she proceeded to tell me that sometimes he just drops by to say, "howdy." No one knows it; he gets no credit for it, but he has been taught to care for his grandmother. The fact is, he does enjoy being with her, but more than that, he realizes her desire to see him, and he is alert to her needs. The leader must not dwell on himself. If he would be independent and self-reliant, he must think of others.

15. *The parent should teach thrift.* Of course, this will teach itself when the child has to work hard for his money; however, there is a certain philosophy to thrift. Thrift enables one to provide for himself when he otherwise would be unable to do so. The one who is not thrifty casts himself upon society and is unfair to his contemporaries. He says, "I will take care of myself now; you take care of me later." The thrifty person says, "I will take care of myself now; I will also take care of myself later."

There is nothing quite so sad as an old man who has made his own way and takes pride in it but at the end of his life is dependent upon someone else. This need not if the child is taught to be frugal when he is young.

16. *As a child grows older he should spend less and less time with the parent; hence, he becomes less and less dependent upon the parent and more dependent upon himself.* He is preparing himself for life and its inevitable decision. He should know of the parents' love and for that matter, maybe he should know why the parent is withdrawing some from him. When the child was very young he was being trained and habits were being formed. When the habits are formed every young person should have opportunity to practice what he has learned. Hence, the teen years can become sort of an internship, where with the supervision of the parent the young person does more and more on his own.

This does not mean the parent should not spend time with the teenager. He should spend time with him, but perhaps they should be briefer periods of time. Activities should be done in which the parent does not obviously excel. There are things which the teenager can do as well or better than the parent. For example, maybe by this time the father and son or mother and daughter are of equal ability at playing ping-pong, bowling, or playing golf.

The warning here is for the parent to give the teenager a little bit of room in which to move, not overly sheltering or protecting him. Yes, the parent should have strict rules concerning morals, principles, punctuality, etc. For example, concerning use of my car, there are set rules as to what David can do and when he can do it. Yet, when the two of us are in the car I usually let him drive. While he is driving I try to refrain from doing "back-seat driving," I let him drive! Then, of course, I let him drive on his own a great deal. Probably he and I are closer this year than we have been in our lives and yet we spend far less time together.

This means that though the parent will not be with the child as much, he does make himself available. He does not interfere with the teenager as long as the rules are being kept. He does not force a conversation on him about his problems at school. He simply makes himself available and lets the young person know that not only is he willing to talk, when and if he is needed, but he is also willing to listen. Much care should be taken here to avoid treating a teenager as if he were a child. The parent should realize he dare not spend too much time with him and that he dare not be overly protective.

Another point should be stressed. Far too many parents spend time with their children only to gratify the parents' desires. A get-together should always be at the discretion of the parent and for the good of the child. It should be administered like medicine, good food, etc. Just the right amount at just the right time should be the goal.

17. *The parent should stress that no one owes anyone else a living.* Yes, our government gives us the opportunity and freedom with which to make a living, but it does not owe us a living. No shiftless or lazy man is honest and no shiftless or lazy man can be independent. One should say, "I am a man! I can act, I can think, I can make my decisions. I will be my own man." This does not mean that one should avoid counsel. Far to the contrary, one should seek counsel and let wiser heads than his advise him. In the final analysis the decisions must be his if he is to become a man of decision.

18. *The parent should not allow idleness.* A child should be taught to avoid hanging around street corners and poolrooms or getting in the car and just idly driving around. Such habits go along with bad resorts: smoking cigarettes, drinking beer and whiskey, and just hanging around in general. Name

me one independent man who was supported by his family while he was young, by his wife and family during the middle years, and by the state when he got old. There is none! How sad! Someone has said, "While the devil tempts all other men, idle men tempt the devil." Another has reminded us, "Even a bicycle falls when it stops."

19. *As the child grows older he should be allowed to buy more and more of his personal belongings.* Perhaps at about the age of ten he could buy his own socks. The parent should tell him what color. Let him decide what kind. When he is about eleven or twelve, with some supervision and instruction he could buy his own shoes. By the time a child is thirteen or fourteen he should be qualified to buy his own clothes. Again, it should be remembered there are boundaries as to style, color, size, etc.

It is almost humorous to go into a men's clothing store and see some little 5'2" mother leading a 6'4" teenage son into the men's department and treating him like he were a three-year-old. She later wonders why the son dosen't hold down a steady job and why he joins a hippie group and in general is a liability to society.

Conclusion: This may be the most important chapter in this book, and certainly apart from Scriptural discipline and spiritual training, it is. Yet, in a real sense, the aforementioned material is a part of spiritual training, for the Bible says that one who provides not for his own is worse than an infidel and that one who does not work should not eat. The Bible does say that each man should be taught to bear his own burden.

Independent, self-reliant, industrious, thrifty, and able adults are not an accident. They are a result of childhood training. This is why the best of us often come from backgrounds of poverty, hardship, and sometimes even tragedy. Let us not let the fact that our young people have not had such incidents prevent them from developing the character that is taught by experiencing them.

Chapter Eight

A CHILD'S RELATIONSHIP WITH OTHERS

Many years ago in the city of London, England, the Salvation Army was conducting its annual convention. General William Booth, the great founder of the Army, was in failing health, had bad eye sight, and was unable to attend the convention. Someone suggested that he send a message to be read at the opening of the convention in order to challenge the hearts of the delegates. This he did. The moderator rose to read the message and this is what he read. "Dear Delegates of the Salvation Army Convention: Others. Signed, General Booth." The successful life must be built around others, and the happy adult must as a child be taught to live for others.

Life has been called a series of relationships. The degree of one's happiness and success in life depends upon his properly relating himself with those of his society with whom he comes in contact. Barrie wrote, "Always be a little kinder than necessary."

Hence, the child should begin early in life adhering to the spirit of the golden rule which is basically expressing goodwill and friendliness to all. From the President to the garbage collector, from the millionaire to the ditch digger, he should be taught to show good manners to all. One becomes a snob when he shows good manners only to those whom he thinks equal or superior to himself in position or wealth. He should be doing what he can to lighten the burdens of others and to make their lives more comfortable. It is interesting how many words include the word "other." Notice the words, "mother," "another," "brother," etc.

1. *Parents.* Since the child is to love his parents, that love will find vent in action. He should be taught to put their interests first, to put their pleasures and comforts before his own, to lift their burdens, to treat them with proper courtesy, and to show interest in them, their needs, and their lives. William Penn wrote, "If thou wouldst be obeyed as a father, be obedient as a son." "Rather the child cry than the mother sigh," is an old saying.

It is sad but true that many parents who have not had formal training are thought to be ignorant or behind the times by their children. Often they are treated with contempt, shame, or at best, indifference. It is true that the parent may not know the latest scientific discoveries or much of history, geography, mathematics, etc., but he has learned from experience and longevity many things that the child must learn in a similar way. Hence, the parent is worthy of the child's respect, love, care, and help. The greatest of Americans have offered such help to their parents. George Washington, Abraham Lincoln, and others have led the way in such obedience and respect.

Children should help their parents. The girls can wash the dishes, clean the house, sew, sweep, dust, care for younger children, dress the younger children, cook, etc. The boys can care for the shining of shoes, cleaning of the sidewalks, shoveling of the snow, mowing of the yard, taking care of pets, etc. All should be done punctually and in order. Children can run errands, help take care of the house, care for parents when they are ill, and in general, show their love and respect by attending to their needs.

Occasionally the parents should have a meeting with the children and discuss with them what they have done lately to help lighten the load of Mom and

Dad. Honor should be given when honor is due and scolding when scolding is due.

There are many reasons why the child owes his parents respect and love. The main one is that he owes a debt to his parents. He owes them for their care for him, their sacrifice, their hard work, etc. The debt which the child owes is a huge one and if he is honest, he must pay it. He should be reminded constantly by his mother concerning the many hours of hard labor his father has put in for the care of the child and to provide for his needs. The mother should stress this contribution by the father and lead the child to realize the tremendous debt he owes. On the other hand, the father should constantly remind the children concerning the debt they owe their mother. They should be reminded of the house cleaning, the sewing, the mending, the travail in birth, the cooking, the washing, the ironing, and the many other contributions made to them by Mother.

There is another reason why parents are due love and respect and that is because they hold a high and noble office. The office of parenthood demands respect regardless of the person who fills it. Children should be taught to respect positions of honor such as president, governor, mayor, principal, pastor, and yes, parent. The parental position deserves the child's respect.

Another reason the child should love and respect his mother and father is that the parents represent God. Someone has said that they are His vicars on earth. The fact that a child is to respect God means that he should be taught to respect His earthly representatives.

Lastly, respect for the parents should be shown and given because of their experience. They may not have studied formally in school, but they have obtained even greater information and in some cases a greater education in the school of experience and wisdom. They may not know the latest methods of pedagogy, but they have struggled, fought, labored sacrificed, worked, and yes, they have even lived longer, and respect should be given to seniority.

The parent who insists on this respect and requires that he is treated courteously and with preference is not being selfish. He is training a child in the way he should go.

2. *Grandparents.* Much stress should be given to proper treatment and respect of grandparents. It is easy to forget them. They are not as young and exciting as they once were. They may seem out of date. Their interests are not those of young people, yet they have made vital contributions to the lives of their grandchildren. The position that they hold warrants love, respect, and attention. They should be visited by their grandchildren. They should receive letters, phone calls, gifts, and special attention from them.

3. *Brothers and sisters.* The relationship between brothers and sisters should be sweet. Much harm has been done by lightly and glibly speaking of how poorly brothers and sisters get along. This sin has promoted such behavior and it is certainly not necessary. Look at the brother relationship that existed between Andrew and Peter, Moses and Aaron, John and Charles Wesley, Dr. John Rice and Dr. Bill Rice, and other great people. Such relationships are begun early in life as children are taught to love each other. They should be taught to share, to avoid jealousy, to praise each other, and to rejoice when the other is praised. The older should provide watchful care over the younger. As more children come into the family the parents naturally have less time to spend with each of them. Consequently, the older children are given the opportunity of caring for the

younger ones. This enables a close relationship to be developed between the children, but it also builds a partnership between older children and the parents. If such care is to be taken when they grow older, they must be taught and reminded from early childhood of the responsibility that will become theirs later. The wise parent teaches this to his first child, and if a larger family is planned, he teaches this to the first several children. He will be glad in his later years that he did.

4. *The teacher.* As children become old enough to go to school they must partially transfer their obedience and respect from home to school and from the parent to the teacher. Bear in mind that the child has been taught to respect authority in government and also the authority of the parents. As he approaches school he must stop to realize that in obeying his teacher he is obeying both the government and the parent. The government has chosen a teacher to be its representative and many of the duties the parent has been performing for the child, the teacher now performs. Hence, to be a good citizen and a good son or daughter requires the child to be an obedient pupil at school. Hence, he should be helpful, respectful, and obedient to the teacher even as he has been to his parents. The ways of expressing this respect are many. The pupil should be kind and helpful. He should not be unruly or misbehave. He must be willing to be thoughtful of younger pupils and to share with his fellow classmates. He must set a good example for those under him. He must work hard, study hard, and do his best to make good grades. He must honor the position of the teacher and accept his leadership, discipline, and assignments. He must be prompt, honest, cooperative and helpful. He must treat his classmates as brothers and his schoolmates as

members of a family. He must learn to live with them in the school community. He must be kind, unselfish, protective, and courteous as he fits into his new environment and his new life.

5. *Society.* Notice that the child's scope of fellowship is increasing. At first he learns the proper relationship and behavior toward his parents, then the entire family, and then his classmates. He is preparing himself to become a serving member of society and, of course, all of the rules of behavior that he has been taught as he relates himself to the aforementioned people must now be transferred to a larger circumference. He must now apply the golden rule to those outside his own home and school. Just as he has obeyed the laws at home and at school, now he obeys the laws in society. He realizes that he must now exercise goodwill to the community and he must keep its laws regardless of the inconvenience it brings to him. He must learn to help this larger family live at its best. Though the laws may hamper him, they are the best for the most. They protect the rights of others to enjoy life to its fullest. Hence, he should be taught to be courteous; to treat the aged properly; and to be patient, quiet, appropriate, inconspicuous, helpful, and discreet. He must not manifest rowdiness, a lack of ettiquette, discourtesy, crowding, pushing, jostling, impatience, etc. A child should be taught fairness in games, putting others before himself. He should be taught not to argue or alibi. He should be taught to wait his turn and share. He should be taught how to behave in places of public entertainment. He should be taught the proper behavior in business transactions and in every proper social situation. He must be taught to care for property such as seats, songbooks, furniture, and equipment that does not belong to him. He must be taught to respect the speed limit.

He should be warned against criticism. talebearing, and gossip. He must be taught to respect age and handicaps. He should be taught to say, "Yes, ma'am," "No, ma'am," Yes, sir," and No, sir." He should be taught to dress appropriately. He should be warned against being loud and overbearing. He should be taught not to be too forward. He should be taught to be discreet and proper in his behavior toward the opposite sex. He should be taught public manners such as giving his seat to an older person. If he is a boy, he should give his seat to a lady or girl if there is none available for her. He should be taught courtesy to public servants such as policemen, firemen, trainmen, doormen, etc. He should be taught to dispose of garbage only in receptacles provided. He should be taught to be quiet, not rough or loud on streets or in public places. He should be taught not to stare at the unfortunate and their deformities. He must be taught to be helpful to strangers and to answer them courteously. He must be taught to help older people as they walk through dangerous places. He must be taught not to whisper, talk, or misbehave in public meetings. He must be taught not to loiter in public places or to hand around restaurants, drive-ins, etc. He must be taught to respect the rights of every man regardless of his color, race, or religion. He must be taught not to deface public property.

In other words, the child must be taught to be a good citizen. Boys should be trained to be gentlemen and girls should be taught to be ladies as they interact with society.

Chapter Nine

THE CHILD AND MONEY

Man's responsibility to his child is not to leave him to live a life of idleness, but rather to equip him to live a life of service. Money is only a certificate that represents service. When a man performs a service he is to receive the appropriate amount of money. When a man has a service done for him, he should pay the proper amount of money representing the value of the service performed. Hence, basically money is simply "time." It represents the amount of time occupied by the service which earned it. No child can develop good character unless he has the proper attitude toward money. Several truths must be taught if this attitude is developed.

1. *Money is not a means of happiness.* A little child is often led to believe that happiness increases when wealth increases. This belief must be combatted, for it is exactly the opposite of the truth. Quite to the contrary, usually the happiness in man diminishes as his wealth increases. To a man who is very poor a small increase can bring a large increase of enjoyment and pleasure. To a man who is very rich, no amount of increase can bring him more happiness. Just a few dollars a month increase in the salary of a poor man may bring him much enjoyment, whereas to a millionaire thousands of dollars added to his estate gives him little enjoyment. One who is going to acquire a lot can have more happiness by acquiring it gradually and by earning it himself. This way he enjoys each step of the trip to success whereas the one who suddenly accumulates much wealth jumps

over many steps of enjoyment.

2. *Money should be a servant, not a master.* There are many perils involved in wealth. One of the greatest of these is the ease with which money can become one's master. Often it possesses the possessor. A little money one can control; it can be his servant. On the other hand, if one has much money, it often controls him and becomes his master.

3. *The important thing in life is not how much one is worth but what one is doing.* It is more important to serve than to increase. What has he done? What is he doing? These are the important questions. How much does he live for others? How much has he given to others? How much has he done for others? How much has he helped others?

Once a man asked John Bright, the English statesman, "Do you know that I am worth a million sterling?" whereupon Mr. Bright replied, "Yes, I do, and I know that is all you are worth."

Themistocles said, "Rather a man without money than money without a man."

Marden said, "Be a millionarie of character instead of a millionarie of money."

4. *The important thing in life is to serve, not to make money.* Money is incidental. Service should be predominant. Most of the truly great men in history have not been men of wealth. Once the country of France voted to determine who was the greatest Frenchman who ever lived. Napoleon and others were bypassed and the French elected Pasteur as their greatest man. Of all the men who received votes not one was a millionaire. Great men such as Lincoln, Washington, Franklin, etc. cared nothing for what they got out of life, but rather for what they put into it and what they could do for others.

To be sure the workman is worthy of his hire, but money should not be the supreme thing. Many years ago when I was just a preacher boy I had to settle this matter in my own heart. I went alone with God and spent an entire evening in prayer. I promised God that I would never discuss money as far as the Lord's work is concerned. I would never ask for any particular remuneration. I would never discuss salary with a church. I promised God that I would trust Him to take care of my needs. He has done so in a wonderful way.

Many great people have turned down more money in order to do more service. Robert E. Lee refused the presidency of an insurance company and its big salary to become President of Washington College with a small salary. Spurgeon refused to come to America to lecture fifty times at $1000 a night. He did this because it would have taken him away from the work God had called him to do. Emerson set his income at a fixed amount and refused to accept any more. The same has been done by other great men such as Chinese Gordon, Pitt, Wellington, Burbank, and others.

One of my dearest friends offered me an apartment house with seven apartments as a gift. The love behind the offer was worth more to me than the apartment house. I politely rejected the gift though the apartment house is probably worth $100,000.

Once a relative offered me a great sum of money and I rejected it. I appreciated the love behind the offer, but did not accept the money. Upon hearing of these two offers and of my rejecting them a friend once asked why I rejected them. I replied that I have always been poor and have always been extremely happy, so I know that I can be poor and be happy. I do not know that I can be rich and be happy. Hence, the safest thing is to retain my poverty, for then I can be sure that I can retain my happiness. Otherwise, it would be a gamble.

In the Koran we find these words: "When a man dies they who survive him ask what property he left behind. The angel bends over the dying man and asks what good deeds he has sent before him."

These truths are pictured so beautifully in the words of Christ Who said, "I came not to be ministered unto, but to minister."

5. *A child should be taught the dangers of betting and gambling.* Show him that the injustice lies in obtaining something for nothing or obtaining money without giving in return an equal amount of service to others. This is the worst thing about gambling. No return is rendered. The prize comes from the pocket of the loser into the pocket of the winner and the loser gets no proper return, allowing the winner to receive that which he did not earn.

Of course, there are other wrongs in gambling, such as the fact that the owner of the establishment arranges it so he is sure to win. There is also the awful tragedy of poverty caused by money wasted and squandered through gambling. Millions of children have gone hungry and millions of families have gone without proper provisions because of this sin.

6. *Much stress should be given to the fact that stealing any item is stealing money.* Children should be taught that when one steals a book, a garment, a toy, or any other item he steals not only the amount of money equivalent to the value of the object, but he also steals the amount of time it would normally take to earn the corresponding amount of money.

The parent should think of as many instances and illustrations of this as he can; for example, the taking of a book, chalk, etc. at school; slipping into an entertainment without paying; taking money from his mother's drawer or his father's billfold, even if he plans to replace it, etc. The parent should think of practically every possible way the child could steal or be dishonest and explain to him that he is stealing money and time from another.

The penalty or punishment inflicted for such offenses should follow the offense quickly. The punishment should never be omitted, should cause more discomfort than the stealing caused comfort, and should be consistent with previous punishment so the child will affix the crime to the penalty and have a definite connection between them. Much emphasis should be placed upon the fact that the sin is the stealing, not how much is stolen or what is stolen. An old saying reminds us, "He who steals a pin will surely steal a greater thing."

The child should be taught that he has been dishonest, for honesty is justice and respect for the rights of others.

7. *The child should always be paid what the service is worth.* Suppose Johnny mows the yard and it takes him thirty minutes. His dad pays him $5 for doing this task. Johnny's labor was not equal to the money he received. He received more money than the service he rendered. He is being taught an unbalanced sense of values, and he will always want to receive money in excess of the service rendered. The father thought he was doing Johnny a favor when in actuality he is doing Johnny a great harm. Such excessive payments are usually not prompted by Johnny anyway, but rather by the parent so as to gain favor with Johnny. Such favor is ill-gotten and exceedingly harmful. The child has a right to the money for the service rendered, but no more.

8. *Excessive allowances to be spent on pleasure, etc. are dangerous.* It is far better for the child to earn what he gets. If a child receives a stipulated amount each week from his parents, he should have regular, routine duties to perform in return for this amount. Now perhaps this allowance should not be spent on

food, clothing, etc. when the child is very young. At that age his allowance should be minimal and he should be encouraged to save much of it. However, with proper guidance he should spend it as he chooses as is mentioned in the chapter on independence.

9. *Children should be taught to tithe.* The giving of at least 1/10 of one's increase should be taught to the child from his infancy. He should give at least 1/10 of every dime that comes into his possession and should form at the earliest possible age the habit of tithing.

The first money that I ever made was on a paper route. When I was ten years of age I began throwing papers for the Dallas Morning News. I would get up at 3:30 in the morning, go get my papers, throw my route, and get back home about 5:00 in time to sleep a bit before going to school. The first week I made $3. My mother sat me down for a conference. She explained to me what she had taught me through the years, that 30 cents of that money was God's and that I had not really given God a penny until I had already given Him His 30 cents. Hence, I laid 30 cents aside and said, "Dear God, this is Yours." I had become a tither. What an ecstasy I felt. What a thrill to be a co-laborer with God and a partner in His wonderful work. This should be the heritage of every child.

10. *Every cent should be spent carefully, preferably on that which is permanent.* A good rule is to spend it only on that which lasts. Candy, chewing gum, cigarettes, carbonated drinks, ice cream, picture shows, etc. shortly pass away and leave nothing in one's hands to show for his money. This is not to say that all of the above-mentioned are wrong; it is simply to say there are things that are more right. Of course, the child will not waste his money as frequently if he earns the money himself. This is why

he should have to earn the money so he will spend it more wisely.

It is also wise for a child to be taught to spend the money for that which gives delight and help to the most people. Bryan wrote, "If thou joy would win, share it; happiness was born a twin." This is just another way to say we should use our money for others.

11. *Children should be taught that they must provide for their parents when they are aged.* This one fact marks one of the main differences between the uncivilized and civilized peoples of this world. When their aged are no longer able to be of service to the uncivilized family they are turned out to die. As civilization increases they are treated with more humanity until among the most civilized people care is provided for the aged.

When my son was two or three years of age I began to drill him to take care of his parents when they become aged. This is the proper thing to do, the Christian thing to do, and yes, the manly thing to do.

12. *The child should be taught to make his own way.* This often presents a problem for the rich child or the child of the successful parent, and of course, there is always the temptation for this type of parent to lead the child to follow in his own footsteps. It would be far better for him to start at the bottom and work his way up. In most cases it is best for the child to enter another profession other than that of his successful parent.

In some cases this is not wise or practical. My son, for example, is going to be a preacher, but I have insisted that he make his own way. A few years ago he was asked to bring a message on a radio broadcast. This was his first sermon. Several folks who heard it told me that it was a good message and that he is a splendid preacher. One dear brother asked if I were

going to let David preach for me now that he had
preached his first sermon. I replied that I was not
going to do so. He then asked, "How do you expect
to make a preacher out of him if you don't let him
preach?"

I replied, "I am not trying to make a preacher out
of him. I am trying to make a man out of him. If I
can make a man of him, God can make a preacher of
him." It is far easier to make a preacher out of a man
than a man out of a preacher.

By all means a child should not be taught that the
world is his. He should not be coddled in his infancy
and allowed to lean upon others. The child that does
this will not develop stamina. He is born with a silver
spoon in his mouth and will become a weakling.

Someone has compared life to a gymnasium. One
never becomes strong or develops strong muscles by
looking at the weights, the parallel bars, etc. He must
use them for himself.

Napoleon once said that he was concerned about
the luxury of the young nobles. He went on to say
that nobody could be successful in life without the
habit of independence and suggested that even the
wealthy be required to clean their own rooms, groom
their own horses, and have their own hardships. It is
tremendously important that every child earn his own
way, make his own mark, be his own man or woman,
and be responsible in a large measure for his own
success.

The Lord Jesus said, *"For where your treasure is,
there will your heart be also."* (Matthew 6:21) How
true! If we would have the hearts of our children
become right, we must have them use their treasure
properly. Alexander Pope once said, "An honest man
is the noblest work of God." Don Quixote said,
"Either live or die with honor. The man without
honor is worse than dead." May God help us to lead

our children to live and die with honor, honesty, and integrity. May they be taught to make their own way and not to become parasites on the government and society for support.

Chapter Ten

READING

Children should be encouraged to read a lot as soon as they have learned to do so. This is one of the most important factors in the rearing of a child. Of course, the wise parent will choose the books that the child reads. Perhaps the best books are biographies. These show what man has done as well as what he can do. They will also encourage the child to imitate great people and identify with them.

For years this author has placed biographies at the very top of his priority list. He has been influenced tremendously by the lives of great men such as Washington, Pasteur, Moody, Garibaldi, Robert E. Lee, Billy Sunday, Charles G. Finney, and others.

The parent may consult his pastor for good reading material for his child. He should also investigate what the child is asked to read in the public schools, or for that matter, in any school. It is the responsibility of the mother and father to see to it that the child reads that which is proper, good, and moral. It is becoming increasingly more necessary for parents to approve every reading assignment that the child receives at the public school. Profane, immoral, and revoluntionary books are required reading by public school teachers. Parents and parent groups should watch very carefully as forces of communism and indecency are making their way into the hearts of American children via the school teacher.

Chapter Eleven

DISCIPLINE AND PUNISHMENT

A generation ago child psychologists came out with the theory that spanking a child may leave him with inner rebellion. They proposed that his desires should not be thwarted. Child psychology courses emphasized this theory. Unconverted professors and Bible-rejecting lecturers joined with misguided authors in spreading the theory that spanking a child would leave him with certain repressed desires and would thwart his progress. Sincere, but deceived parents and educators swallowed this poison. Hence, we did not spank the child's hands when he did wrong. We took the paddle out of the schoolroom and the bite out of the law. Those unspanked children are now grown. Whereas they were throwing vases in living rooms, they are now throwing stones through store-front windows. Whereas they were lighting matches in kitchens, now they are setting fires to shopping centers, R.O.T.C. buildings, and banks. Whereas they were holding baby brothers hostage in basements, they are now holding principals and college presidents hostage in administration buildings. Whereas they were rebelling against mothers and fathers, now they are rebelling against God and country. Whereas parents would not force them to bathe when they could have done so, now society cannot make them bathe as adults. Because they were not forced to dress properly as children, they will not dress properly nor assume responsibility in society now.

These prophets of anarchy taught us that spanking

a child would cause the child to hate the parents. Now these unspanked children, who are supposed to love their parents, embrace a philosophy whose first premise is hatred and even a willingness to kill Mother and Father, but the young folks who were spanked as children and disciplined in adolescence have a love for their aging parents that is envied by those who were deceived by these pseudopsychologists.

Headed by their messiah, who was a leading children's physician, and inspired by his disciples who led this movement in the schoolroom, the followers of this heresy accused the Bible-believers of ruling by force and not by love. They included in their gospel such foolish statements as, "I love my boy to much to whip him," etc. They refused to accept God's admonition in Proverbs 13:24, *"He that spareth his rod hateth his son: but he that loveth him chasteneth him betimes."* In Hebrews 12:6 we read, *"For whom the Lord loveth He chasteneth, and scourgeth every son whom He receiveth."* Now we face a generation of anarchy, rebellion, and yes, even revolution which has been sown in doctors' offices, classrooms, and nurseries by such tools as typewriters, office pens, and the silver tongues of orators.

Since disregarding the Word of God concerning discipline has led us to arrive at our present destination, let us seek the reversal of such a trend by examining the Scriptures and heeding them.

The Bible is clear that little children are born in sin. Psalm 51:5, *"Behold, I was shapen in iniquity; and in sin did my mother conceive me."* Psalm 58:3, *"The wicked are estranged from the womb; they go astray as soon as they be born, speaking lies."* Because of this God has given parents to children to discipline them, to spank them, and to teach them the awful results of wrong. The plain teaching of the Scripture is that the parent who disciplines his child does both child and parent a great favor. Let us notice these favors.

1. *The parent who spanks the child teaches him to have wisdom.* Proverbs 29:15, *"The rod and reproof give wisdom: but a child left to himself bringeth his mother to shame."* The child is taught the wisdom that sin does not pay and that it brings displeasure, discomfort, and heartache. He will learn to associate wrong with punishment and thereby flee from it.

2. *The parent who spanks his child provides himself with a happy future.* Proverbs 29:15b, *"....but a child left to himself bringeth his mother to shame."* Oh, the heartbreak endured by parents who have failed to discipline their children. Many such are decaying in old folks' homes across the nation and around the world. They sit by silent telephones and search through empty mail boxes made so by the ungrateful child whose life is bringing shame and reproach to Mother and Dad. While these lovely souls pine their hearts away in remorse, their old-fashioned counterparts enjoy security, protection, provision, and love from those whom they spanked and disciplined as children.

3. *The parent who spanks his child guarantees him a clean life.* Proverbs 20:30, *"The blueness of a wound cleanseth away evil: so do stripes the inward parts of the belly."* In other words, the parent who disciplines cleanses the child from evil character and inward sin. The child has been taught that sin brings trouble. He learns to fear and hate it. Someday he will rise and call his parents blessed.

4. *The parent who spanks his child offers for himself more opportunities for service to God.* In writing to Timothy in I Timothy 3:4, 5 Paul says that a pastor should be one who *"ruleth well his own house, having his children in subjection with all gravity; (For if a man know not how to rule his own*

house, how shall he take care of the church of God?)" He also disqualifies from the office of deacon one who does not control his children properly. I Timothy 3:12, *"Let the deacons be the husbands of one wife, ruling their children and their own houses well."* Hence, one who does not follow God's plain teaching about discipline is not qualified to hold either of the offices in the New Testament church. God will not use men who disobey Him in this vital matter. One reason God blessed Abraham so mightily is the fact that he could trust him to *"command his children and his household after him,"* according to Genesis 18:17-19.

Eli, the high priest in the days of Samuel, forfeited great blessings from God because he did not properly discipline his sons. His two sons, Hophni and Phinehas, were both wicked men. In I Samuel 3:12-14 we have God's judgment upon him. Notice very carefully in verse 13 the words, *"because his sons made themselves vile, and he restrained them not."* Judgment fell upon Eli and upon his house because he did not discipline his sons.

5. *The disciplining parent adds years to the life of his child.* Exodus 20:12, *"Honour thy father and thy mother: that thy days may be long upon the land which the Lord thy God giveth thee."* What a favor the parent has done to the child when he disciplines and spanks him. He literally adds years to his life.

6. *Such a parent guarantees his own child a happy old age.* The Bible teaches in Proverbs 22:6, *"Train up a child in the way he should go: and when he is old, he will not depart from it."* In other words, when the child is away from home without the presence of the discipline of his mother and father, he will not depart from his training. He will become a happy and prosperous member of society and will be a properly adjusted adult. This Scripture should be observed

very carefully. Many parents of children who have gone into deep and terrible sin comfort themselves in the fact that the child will come back because Proverbs 22:6 promises it. This is not the teaching here! The Bible never promises that a child who goes off in deep sin will come back, but rather teaches that a child reared properly will never depart from the way he has been trained. In other words, it does not say, "he will come back to what he has been taught," but rather it says, "he will not depart from what he has been taught."

7. *The parent who corrects his child will probably save the life of the child.* Proverbs 23:13 says, *"Withhold not correction from the child: for if thou beatest him with the rod, he shall not die."* Now at first reading we might be led to believe that the teaching of this verse is that the rod itself will not kill the child and certainly this is true if administered properly, but there is another teaching here: The child who has been spanked and taught that doing wrong brings bad results, tragedy, and punishment will less likely brawl or be killed in a car wreck because of drinking while driving. He is not as likely to die of some terrible disease caused by sin. In other words, he will be taught to live a safer life than he would have lived had he not been disciplined. Ah, how fortunate is such a one.

8. *The parent who spanks the child keeps him from going to hell.* Proverbs 23:14, *"Thou shalt beat him with the rod, and shalt deliver his soul from hell."* A child who is spanked will be taught that there is a holy God Who punishes sin and wrong. Hence, he will learn to heed authority and obey the laws and rules. When he then hears the Word of God he will obey what he hears and will accept the Gospel as it is preached. The parent has kept his child from hell by teaching him truths that can be learned only

by discipline and the use of the rod.

9. *The spanking parent teaches his child how to equip himself better for the future, for he will obtain a better education.* When the child has been taught to respect authority, obet the rules, and keep the laws before he starts to school he then transfers this obedience and respect to his school teacher. Because of this he receives a better education, better equips himself for life, and will be of more value to society and reap a larger financial reward. Hence, the parent who disciplines his child Scripturally is putting money in his pocket and success in his future.

Many parents are willing to abide by the aforementioned principles, yet do not have the knowledge of the practical side of administering such discipline. Some practical suggestions follow:

1. *Let the child realize that you are simply representing God in the execution of the punishment.* Explain to him that parents represent God before their children and that they are ministers to execute His judgment. Psalm 103:13 says, *"Like as a father pitieth his children, so the Lord pitieth them that fear Him."* So God is like a father and He chooses fathers and mothers to represent Him in the punishing of little children. Let the child realize that if you as a parent do not punish him properly, you are being disobedient to God and committing the same sin the child is committing. Explain to him that you are a child of God and if you refuse to obey God in the execution of His judgment upon your children, God will pour out His wrath upon you. For you to be a good child of God requires that you be a good parent to the child. Let him understand this. He will get the idea that God is a holy and just God, One Who loves and yet One Who wants us to become our best. For this to be so He must punish us when we are deserving.

2. *Sometimes spanking should leave stripes on the child.* Proverbs 20:30 says, *"The blueness of a wound cleanseth away evil; so do stripes the inward parts of the belly."* Our natural man rebels at such punishment, but we are reminded in I Corinthians 2:14 that the natural man cannot understand the things of the Spirit. Hence, we have to trust the God Who knows more than we and obey Him.

I can well recall when I was a boy we had a peach tree in the back yard. I do not ever recall seeing a peach grow on that tree. When I think of the old peach tree I think of Mother walking back from it with a branch in her hand, peeling the leaves off as she came. I then recall her using that switch to spank my little bare legs. I can still see the stripes often left by that switch, and I thank God for every one of them. Today I call her "blessed" because of her faithfulness to the teaching of God and her willingness to obey Him. Placing stripes on me as a child kept me from bearing more painful ones as an adult. Ephesians 6:4 says, *"And, ye fathers. . .bring them up in the nurture and admonition of the Lord."* The word "nurture" means "chastening." It is the same word that is used concerning the scourging of Christ as He was beaten with the cat-o'-nine-tails. The wise and spiritual parent obeys God and follows His commandments, not his own reason.

3. *Begin early in spanking the child.* Susannah Wesley said she spanked John and Charles before they were a year old. Certainly the wise parent will start by at least this age. Proverbs 19:18 says, *"Chasten thy son while there is hope, and let not thy soul spare for his crying."* This means there is a time in a child's life when no hope is left. During the formative years, yea, the infant years, the child should be spanked. As soon as he is old enough to walk away from his parents he should be spanked if he does not walk

where they say he should walk. As soon as he is old enough to understand what they say he should be spanked if he disobeys what they say. This Scripture admonishes us that even when a child is so young that his crying reaches our sympathy, and though it is hard for us as compassionate parents to spank one who seems so innocent, we should nevertheless discipline him. Parents should not have to remove vases and delicate glass ornaments from living room tables. A house need not become disorderly and full of riots because a baby has come. Start early in disciplining the child.

4. *The parent should build such a close relationship that the worst part of the spanking is the broken fellowship between the child and parent.* I can still recall how disappointed my mother's face looked when she spanked me and I can recall how I dreaded displeasing her even more than I dreaded the spanking, (and believe me, I DID dread the spanking). When the love and affection is close between the child and parent and the relationship is what it ought to be, the worst part of a whipping is the broken fellowship. In other words, when the parent is not disciplining, the relationship should be so wonderful, the fellowship so sweet, and life so happy that the severance of that in itself is terrible punishment for the child to endure.

5. *The spanking should be a ritual.* No mother or father should jerk the child up and in a fit of temper administer a spanking. In fact, no punishment should ever be given in a fit of temper. The ritual should be deliberate and last at least ten or fifteen minutes. (In the long run time will be saved using this method.) It should be a ritual dreaded by the child. He should not only dread the pain but the time consumed in the ordeal.

6. *The punishment should always be far in excess*

of the pleasure enjoyed by doing the wrong. The child should realize he will always be the loser by far and that the discomfort will be so multiplied that soon he will have forgotten the pleasure derived from the wrong.

7. *The parent should state very clearly to the child the wrongs and the punishment for each one.* As near as possible these wrongs should be listed with the punishment that is to be inflicted for each one. If the punishment does not seem to correct it, then perhaps it should be increased. Some parents have made lists of possible wrongs and have carefully gone over this list with the child explaining exactly what each punishment would be. The punishment is inflicted without exception so that the child will know exactly what to expect.

8. *Before punishing the child tell him clearly what wrong he has committed.* Talk sternly and deliberately without a display of temper. Let him know exactly what he has done wrong. Then require that he state to you exactly what the wrong was so that what he did is very clear to you and to the child. Then, ask him what the punishment is. By this time he will know. Let him know that to be just and righteous you must inflict the punishment reminding him that you are doing it in the place of God against Whom he has really sinned.

9. *Never give a child that for which he cries.* The baby who cries for attention and gets it will become a child who cries for a toy and gets it, then a teenager who whines and complains for his every whim and gets it, and then a young adult who will demonstrate and riot in order to get his wishes. Riots are not started in the streets but in the crib.

10. *The spanking should be administered firmly.* It should be painful and it should last until the child's will is broken. It should last until the child is crying,

not tears of anger but tears of a broken will. As long
as he is stiff, grits his teeth, holds on to his own will,
the spanking should continue.

11. *After the spanking tell him why you did it.*
While he is still crying have him sit down. Explain to
him again what the crime was and that you had no
alternative but to obey God and punish him for the
crime. Ask him again to repeat to you what he did
that was wrong. Allow the impression of the
association between the wrong and the penalty to be
cut deep in his mind.

Then the wise parent should assure the child of his
love and explain the reason he spanked him was
because of that love. He should then have the child
remain in the room alone. (All spankings should be
administered in privacy and with a closed door.) The
parent should have a brief prayer with the child. Lead
him to realize his sin was really against God. Ask the
child to pray asking God to forgive him. He should
then have time to be alone in the room to think over
his wrong for a few minutes. After two to five
minutes the parent may open the door and allow
normal activity to resume.

12. *Parents should always support each other in
the disciplining of the children.* Sometimes the
mother may think the father is too harsh or too
mean. Sometimes the father may think the mother is
illogical or unreasonable. Such feelings should never
be expressed openly. (Perhaps a discussion can be
carried on privately, though in some cases this would
not be advisable.)

Sometimes older teenagers say to me, "Brother
Hyles, at our house we have two sets of rules: my
mother's and my father's." This causes frustration in
a child's life. The ideal situation would be for the
mother and father to agree on what is wrong and
what punishment should be inflicted. If this is not

possible, there should certainly be support for each other on the part of each parent. It is always best for the parent to be on the side of authority, hence, stripping the child of his desire to seek sympathy from one parent after punishment is meted out by another.

Happy in old age is the parent who obeys God in these matters. Happy is the child who feels the security of such punishment. When Becky, my oldest daughter, graduated from high school and was preparing to go to college, I took her out to eat. I asked her how she was going to rear her children. She looked at me and said, "Dad, exactly as you have reared me." When I asked her why she replied, "Dad, I always knew you loved me when you said, 'No!' "

Chapter Twelve

TELLING THE TRUTH

1. *Teach the child the awful reasons for lying.*
    (1) *Cowardice.* One is afraid to face the consequences of his acts.
    (2) *Personal gain.* This is terrible dishonesty!
    (3) *Malice.*
Teach the child how terrible it is not to tell the truth. I can recall hearing Dr. John Rice telling when the truth became so important to him. He was just a little fellow about five years of age when he told something that wasn't true. His mother became so disappointed and made such a big issue out of it that Dr. Rice felt he had committed some awful crime. He wondered if he could ever be forgiven or if he would have to be sent away to an institution. The importance of telling the truth was impressed so strongly upon his little mind and the awfulness of telling something that wasn't true was emphasized so greatly that he never got away from it, even 70 years later. The wise parent will stress over and over the awfulness of untruth and the importance of truth.

2. *The child should realize the terrible injury that will be upon him when he lies.* The lie hurts the liar more than the one to whom he lies. Much stress should be placed on the fact of facing the father of lies. When one lies he is working in direct partnership with Satan himself. The child should be told what happens to liars. One lie becomes another, then that becomes a bigger one, until finally the penitentiary is filled with people who began lying in childhood.

3. *Stress should be placed upon the fact that lying*

is being a bad member of the team. Compare society with a ball game. Emphasize the disdain the rest of the team has for a particular member who fails to do his best. When one lies he thinks against a society which is built on the confidence, truth, and honesty of the team members. When one lies he hurts the rest of the team and jeopardizes their happiness and success in life.

4. *The parent should insist upon exactness in the reporting of an event.* This must be so regardless of how small the item may seem. Insistence should be made as to accuracy concerning every detail. There should be no differentiating between white lies and black lies, little lies and big lies. All lies are big and all lies are black!

The child should be trained to pay attention. Here is the reason why many people say things that are not true. Especially is this true in the life of children. Inaccurate statements are made because the mind is occupied with other things and one is not perceptive. Hence, from early childhood one must be trained to be attentive and to grasp all that is going on within the realm of possibility.

Play a little game in which each member of the family tells what he saw on a previous occasion or event. Discuss the incidents that took place. Be sure that as many details as possible are retained and that there is agreement about what happened. This can be made into an interesting game. With small children, a prize could be given to the one who remembered the most details and was the most observant.

Teach the child not to say, "I think." This is a dangerous habit for anyone. Someone has said that knowledge is the basis of accuracy. When a question of fact is asked the child should not say. "I think." He should say, "I do not know," or he should be accurate in answering. Such words could be used as "approximately," but this is not good for habit.

5. *Much stress should be placed on keeping one's word.* Emphasize the fact that promises are to be binding. They are very sacred. To break one is stealing. It is lying. It is dishonesty. It is breaking a trust.

6. *Much attention should be given to the fact that lies can be told in other ways than by words.* Here at First Baptist Church of Hammond we have a deaf department. These people cannot hear and they do not speak. Can they lie? Can they tell untruths? It is also true that those of us who can talk and hear can be untruthful without actually speaking words audibly.

7. *Cheating on tests is lying.* The student is telling the teacher that the material he turns in is his. Since it is not his he is guilty of untruth. How awful this is!

8. *Every child should be taught to avoid slander and gossip.* One of the commandments says, *"Thou shalt not bear false witness against thy neighbor."* (Exodus 20:16) The wise man said, *A good name is rather to be chosen than great riches."* (Proverbs 22:1a) Each person has a right to a good name. When we carelessly and idly talk about others we are tempted to enlarge into that which is not true, and for that matter, many times stories are sincerely told wrongly which damage many people.

Play the game of "gossip" with your child. Write out a little incident. Read it one day to a child. Have him tell it the next day to another member of the family and have that one tell it to another. Continue until it is passed through the entire family. The last one tells it as it reached him. Compare it with the first account pointing out the danger of idle talk. Remind the child that people who repeat a slander and gossip are not respectable. People will soon avoid them and be afraid to trust them. Hence, it is to the child's own interest not to become a gossip. Teach him to fill his life with good things. Teach him to read and think for himself, to stay busy, and never to repeat the casual remarks of others. Advise him that the words "he said" and "she said" are words never to be used, for as someone has said, "They are little hinges to the gates of gossip."

9.   *Every child should be taught to pay his debts on time.* As is mentioned in other chapters one who is late in paying a debt is dishonest for the amount of time he is late. Stress over and over and over again the importance of being punctual in paying debts.

10. *Promptness should be strongly emphasized.* If a child promises his mother to be home at a certain time, he should keep the promise. The life of the child who is taught promptness will be far richer and happier because he has learned to keep his word.

The wise parent will drill his child on truthfulness, will teach him the high esteem of this virtue, and will lead him to become an adult who can be trusted and respected in his dealings with others.

Chapter Thirteen

CARE FOR THE BODY

In I Corinthians 6:19 and 20 Paul says, *"What ? know ye not that your body is the temple of the Holy Ghost which is in you, which ye have of God, and ye are not your own? For ye are bought with a price: therefore glorify God in your body, and in your spirit, which are God's."* In Romans 12:1 he says, *"I beseech you therefore, brethren, by the mercies of God, that ye present your bodies a living sacrifice, holy, acceptable unto God, which is your reasonable service."* Hence, the body is a sacred thing to God, and it should be so to the child. Health is not just the business of the individual. When one is sick he causes inconvenience to the entire family and to all those in his little world. Somebody must care for him when he is sick; hence, he incapacitates at least one other person. Not only does he lose the services he performs to himself, but he causes those whom he serves to lose his services. Then also he runs the risk of giving his disease to the one who attends him. Then too, often someone has to finance him and care for his material needs while he is sick. Perhaps he is fortunate enough to have a generous and kind employer who will pay him while he is ill. If improper care of the body caused the illness, he is doing his employer an injustice. Certainly not the least important fact is that it is only with our bodies that we can serve God. It matters not how spiritual we are, how alert our minds, or how warm our hearts, when our bodies are sick we cannot serve our Lord properly. Because of these and other things the child should be taught to care for his body. The following rules are good ones for him to follow:

1. *Eat properly.* As a man eats so is he. The physical and nervous energy depend largely on how and with what the body is fed. In order to eat properly one must be moderate in eating fats and sugars. In fact, I would suggest eating only raw sugar. He should avoid the use of alcohol and tobacco. He should avoid highly spiced foods, pickles, sauces, pastries, etc. He should drink at least three pints of water during the day. He should eat food as nearly as God prepared it as possible. For example, he should eat nuts instead of "snick-snacks," fruit instead of candy, fruit juices instead of carbonated drinks, and simple vegetables (raw as often as possible) instead of highly seasoned mixtures of food. The child should be taught that a car will not run properly with too much gasoline or bad gasoline. The body cannot run as well with an excess of food or with improper food. Hence, having the proper diet and not overeating should be strongly stressed. It is my opinion that every family should become acquainted with a good health food store and eat as near to nature as possible.

2. *Fresh air is important in the building of a strong body.*

3. *Proper exercise is necessary.* Exercise not only increases the strength and size of the muscles but more important, it keeps the circulation of the blood normal in the different parts of the body. By it the heart is developed and strengthened, the lungs are better supplied with oxygen, a better appetite is enjoyed, and the food is better digested. Everyone should have at least thirty minutes of vigorous exercise a day, but this should neither precede nor follow a meal.

It is said that Theodore Roosevelt was a very weak

child but he exercised himself and lived in the out-of-doors in order to gain almost perfect health while he was yet a young man.

4. *The child should get proper sleep.* Children twelve and under should have about ten hours sleep. It, is important that this sleep be as early as possible. It is better to retire early and rise early than to retire late and rise late. Sleep should not follow any meal. In fact, it is usually better to go to sleep on an empty stomach giving the heart rest through the night. It is also a good idea to have some kind of schedule as far as sleep is concerned. If possible, a regular time of retiring and rising is best.

5. *Cleanliness is vital to good health.* I think it is best for a child to have a daily bath, to dry himself vigorously, to wash his face several times a day giving special attention to the cleansing of the ear and nose. The fingernails should be kept very clean. The feet should be washed every night before retiring, and proper habits of personal cleanliness should be developed and practiced. Of course, this should be added to cleanliness at home. Dirty homes, soiled walls, dirty yards, excessive garbage, and decaying food all are sources of infection. We owe it to our neighbors to be clean. Someone has said, "If my neighbor's uncleanliness creates a poisonous atmosphere or conditions that menace my health, he will risk my freedom to live just as much as if he went about it with a pistol." He violates the commandment, "Thou shalt not kill."

6. *Special care should be taken to warn the child of the effects of alcoholic beverages.* Acquaint him with heroes in history who were teetotalers. Drive him to skid row and show him some drunks as they stagger down the street. Remind him that no one intends to be a drunkard when he begins to drink; when he takes his first drink he does not intend to

make it a habit. Teach him that no one ever became an alcoholic without taking his first drink at one time.

It is said that Mr. Lincoln once received several baskets of wine from some friends who felt the city of Springfield had been honored. He returned the gift but thanked them for the kindness.

At one time at New Salem he had a business partner who insisted they sell liquors. Mr. Lincoln withdrew from the partnership.

In 1846 he spoke at a temperance rally in Springfield, Illinois. After he had spoken he offered the following pledge: "Whereas, the use of alcoholic liquors as a beverage is productive of pauperism, degradation and crime, and believing it is our duty to discourage that which produces more evil than good, we therefore pledge ourselves to abstain from the use of intoxicating liquors as a beverage."

Repeatedly Mr. Lincoln refused to have liquor in the White House. Find other great heroes who refused to drink or sell liquor. Remind your children of their total abstinence.

7. *Every child should be warned of the danger of cigarettes.* They should be reminded that the use of nicotine affects one's eyesight, causes diseases of the throat, and affects the heart circulation, the nervous system, etc. Tell the child that Dr. Kellogg of Battle Creek, Michigan, once removed the nicotine from one cigar, placed it in a little water, and injected it into a frog. The frog died instantly. It is said that a chemist tried this same experiment on a cat. The cat died within fifteen minutes. It is said that some dogs have been killed by the injection of one drop of nicotine. Teach the child to fear its deadly effects.

By proper teaching a child can have a longer and more useful life for God and for others. Much care should be taken to teach him that by proper eating, proper exercise, proper rest, and proper hygiene his life can be more fruitful and he can be of better service to mankind. In my book BLUE DENIM AND LACE I make this statement: "With my body I serve you and with my mind I love you. Hence, I pledge to keep a healthy mind that I may love you more and a healthy body that I may serve you better." Not only does a child owe it to himself but to his parents, to his future children, and to his friends to keep his body healthy. The greatest debt, however, is to his God Who owns his body and bought it with a price.

Chapter Fourteen

DISPELLING FEARS

An old Chinese proverb says, "Cowards die many times before they are dead." Shakespeare said, "The valiant never taste death but once." Emerson wrote, "Fear always springs from ignorance." In order to rear a happy and well-adjusted child parents must first face the reality of fears in a child's life.

There are two types of fears to be faced. First, there are some fears that are unavoidable and are common to all people. The child should be taught that there is no shame in feeling such fears. It is not wrong to feel fear; one cannot help the feeling. The wrong lies in yielding to it and not allowing the will to control the action. Feeling is not under the control of the will; yielding to that feeling is. It is the will that controls actions. Hence, when one is a coward it is because he has a weak will. (Note the chapter on SELF–CONTROL.) There is no doubt in the mind of this author but the Shadrach, Meshach and Abednego were afraid of the fiery furnace and that Daniel was afraid of the lion's den. They no doubt felt a feeling of fear, but their actions were not controlled by their feelings. Their actions were controlled by their wills. Hence, a child should be taught that there is nothing wrong in being afraid if he does what he ought to do and if his will decides what he does even in the face of fear.

The second issue that must be faced is the presence of unnecessary fears. One emphasis in this chapter is to teach the parent to teach the child how to eliminate and avoid unnecessary fears. There are many undesirable companions that associate with fear. Fear, we are told, often destroys the white corpuscles of the blood until one's resistance is made low and he can no longer effectively fight the germs of diseases. Medical science teaches that courageous people are not as likely to contact diseases, especially contagious ones. Medical papers once reported a man whose heart was giving forth a peculiar sound. He felt he was suffering from heart disease. He became so weak that he had to call for a doctor. Upon examination the doctor found that the peculiar rasping sound was caused by the man's suspenders on the left side. They were defective and caused the sound. As soon as the man learned of the cause, he recovered!

Now let us notice some common fears and ways to help a child face the inevitable ones and eliminate or avoid unnecessary ones.

1. *Fear of darkness.* Most of us at one time or another have feared to be alone in the dark. This is a fear that is cultivated and is certainly not necessary. Many parents cultivate and perhaps even create such a fear by creating imaginary creatures who live in the darkness. Oftentimes we teach our children by disciplining them improperly that certain evils and wicked powers live in the darkness. We talk to them about the bogeyman who will get them if they are bad. We teach them fairy tales which often associate horrible creatures with the darkness.

A good way to combat this is to imagine that good people live in the darkness. Teach your child stories in which helpful beings lurk in the dark. (Be sure to be honest with the child and let him know it is only a fairy tale.)

The wise parent will think of a lot of things a child can do in the dark. On a summer night let him lie on a pallet in the yard with the parents nearby. The parents could go inside for a drink of water and stay for a about a minute showing the child he can be in the darkness alone. Let the child hunt what we used to call lightning bugs.

The parent should also show the child the beauty of the nighttime. Dwell on the beauty of twilight. Teach him to look at the stars and the moon and to watch the beauties of the heavens. Make him acquainted with the Big Dipper, the Little Dipper, the Milky Way, Mars, etc. In other words, teach the child to enjoy nighttime.

2. *Fear of being alone.* This also is needless fear. It is one that is cultivated and can certainly be avoided. Again there are several things that can be done. First, when the child is just a baby let him be alone. When a baby is just a few days old he learns whether or not he can get extra attention. He finds whether or not a cry or whimper will get somebody to come to his side. If the baby is not sick and not uncomfortable, he should be left alone even if he cries. The crying baby should be examined by the wise parent. If there is no obvious discomfort such as being stuck by a diaper pin, the parent should leave the child to himself. When the child gets a little older the parent may choose to go out into the yard for thirty seconds leaving the child in the house alone. This period of time could be increased, though the parent should perhaps watch from the window to see the very young child is all right. The idea is to let him feel alone and get the habit of realizing it is not bad to be alone.

One of the main reasons children are afraid to be alone is thay they dread silence. When other people are around the noises they make seem to offer a sense of security. When we are alone not only do we not hear noises of others, we also hear noises that we do not normally hear such as the moaning of the wind, the warping of the woodwork, the sound of the cricket, etc. Hence, it is wise for a child to be taught to make noise himself while he is alone. He can do some work that will require noise. He can hammer, saw, or make some other noise so the absence of the noise of others will not be missed and the presence of undesirable noises will not be heard. A good habit is to sing or read aloud when alone. Many times the fear of being alone is simply the fear of being in silence. If nothing else, the radio or television can be played. At any rate, the child should be taught not to be afraid to be alone. It is alarming how many adults are afraid to be alone, especially so during the night hours.

3. *Fear of storms.* Here is a fear that is easily cultivated and that is difficult to prevent. It is a very real one in the life of the child and the parent must be more diligent with the expelling and avoiding of this one than those previously mentioned. One important thing to remember is that the time for teaching lessons concerning storms and alleviating their fears is during good weather. During the storm is no time to teach a lesson on fear of storms. When the weather is calm, the sun is bright and shining, and the skies are clear, the parents should teach their child not to be afraid of storms. Pick out some beautiful day and tell the child the cause of storms, the good they accomplish. Show him weather maps. Convince and assure him that the danger of an electric shock is already over after the flash has been seen. Assure him that the building is protected by lightning rods, etc. Explain that the rods convey the electric shock to the ground. Someone has said that ignorance is the mother of fear. Therefore, take the child to the lightning rods and show him they are in perfect condition. Teach him how they work. Assure him that every precaution has been taken for his safety.

Teach him where the dangerous places are during storms so he can find a safe place.

The wise parent will plan some exciting activity for the child during a storm so as to take his mind off the supposed danger. It might even be wise to point out the beauties of the storm while it is in progress.

Of course, the most important thing is to teach children that God will care for them. Have them memorize Scriptures that will give strength, such as Psalm 91. Lead them in quoting such Scriptures during the storm.

4. *Fear of pain.* Here is a fear that is found in varying degrees in all of us and such a fear can control the will if it is improperly developed or is too weak. In infancy a child should not be held too delicately. This is not to say the parent should be rough with the baby. Quite to the contrary! As he grows he should certainly not be treated like a piece of delicate china. As soon as possible he should be taught to play games that require physical activity and vigorous use of the body. He should form the habit of doing exercises that require physical discomfort and perspiring. Then as soon as possible the boy should engage in contact sports such as football, basketball, baseball, etc. He should feel the jar of the tackle, the discomfort of a fall, the pain of a skinned thigh (we used to call those "strawberries" when we were boys), and the jolts of competition.

When injuries come the child should feel that the parent cares and is concerned about his safety, but that pain is a part of life and that he must learn to bear his own burden without being spoiled by too much sympathy from others. Again courage in such cases depends on the strength of the will as is given in the chapter on SELF—CONTROL. A child when is pain can cry or he can show the strength of his will by a smile. The proper will in a child can force him to do what he ought to do even when in pain. Teach him he can endure pain with a smile like a hero or be weak like a coward.

Tell the child stories of great men who did great things while in pain. Make heroes of Robert Louis Stevenson, who was an invalid all his life but bore his pain with gentleness and optimism. Tell him of many heroes who fought the battle in spite of pain. Acquaint him with Elizabeth Barrett, who was an invalid; and Louisa May Alcott, who wrote AN OLD—FASHIONED GIRL with one arm in a sling, a terrible headache, and no voice. Teach him about John Bunyan, who wrote PILGRIM'S PROGRESS on milk bottle stoppers delivered to him while he was in prison suffering for having preached the Gospel.

Teach him new ways of expressing pain. Do not allow him to whine. Some people whistle when they hurt. Some people have a favorite song they begin to sing. Such expressions may mean that the child is actually complaining, but it will not be interpreted as such by others and they will not excessively sympathize with him and spoil him.

Of course, the wise parent will set the example. If the parent fears nothing but doing wrong, the fears of the children will also be alleviated. Children love to imitate parents. Let them see that the parent has courage in a storm, does not scream or jump on a chair when a mouse runs through the room, is not afraid of the dark, etc. The child will imitate the behavior of the parent.

5. *Fear of emergency.* The child's mind should be trained to be ready in time of danger. He should be taught what to do in times of emergency so that by reflex he will do what is best.

This can be done by discussing with the child possible disasters and giving him a few seconds to answer what he would do in such an emergency. Ask this over and over again and let him answer it repeatedly so the response to a crisis will be automatic.

The wise parent will also let his child participate in activities that require quick decisions. Games such as basketball, ice hockey, etc. are good.

The child should be allowed to act under pressure. When some small crisis arises, the child should be allowed to make his own decision without interference of the overprotective parent.

The child should be drilled in certain emergency practices. The parent should lead the child in supposing that someone is breaking in the house. The child rushes to the phone and dials the police (with his finger on the receiver, of course). Similar situations should be acted out until the child will be properly rehearsed in knowing exactly what to do. This is the psychology behind a fire drill at school. There should be other drills teaching a child exactly what to do when a crisis arises. He will then be able to "keep his cool" under any circumstance.

6. *Fear of being different*. Here is a little imp that lurks in all of us. Early in a child's life he should be taught to doubt and question. He should be taught that it should be his will and not the following of the crowd that makes his decisions. Teach him to suspicion the crowd. Show him that following the crowd is basically slavery. Warn him to keep out of a mob. Someone has said, "A man who deliberately joins a mob confesses two things: that he has secret impulses of evil to which he wishes to give rein, and that he is a coward seeking the shelter of numbers to shield him from the consequences of his crimes." Warn him about joining gangs. Many a child has stolen peaches from an orchard, insulted someone who is less fortunate, done impish pranks on Halloween, etc. just because he was part of a gang.

Especially warn the child to hate the word "let's." He should be warned to suspicion anyone who says, "Let's do so-and-so." The child should be taught that he should exercise his own will, not the mass will of a gang or the crowd. James Bryce said, "There are many echoes but few voices." Theodore Roosevelt said, "Man must have a master. If he is not his own master, someone else will be."

Lead your child to make heroes of men who have not followed the crowd, but have been their own wills. Make heroes of Martin Luther, Benjamin Franklin, and others. Remind the child that no one who did things because others did them has his name indelibly imprinted in the pages of history for his greatness. They used their own minds, were guided by their own consciences, and exercised their own wills. The world may laugh or scorn. The world may criticize or condemn, but they were their own men and though they wanted to please, there were other things they wanted more than to please. Often when a strong person of conviction refuses to follow the crowd, the crowd will follow him.

7.   *Fear of superstition.* Many children are so superstitious that life is filled with unnecessary fears. They are told too many stories of ghosts and witches and are taught to fear them by parents who zealously and yet wrongly discipline. The wise parent will lead his child to avoid such superstitions as being afraid of a black cat or crossing the street, being superstitious about the number 13 or the day Friday. Teach him that Columbus, who discovered American was born on Friday; Washington was born on Friday as were Tennyson, Dickens, Michelangelo, and others. The Battle of Bunker Hill occurred on Friday, June 17, 1775. The English surrendered at Yorktown on Friday, October 18, 1781. The union of the colonists was made on Friday, May 20, 1775. The Mayflower

disembarked its first persons on American soil on Friday, and it landed at Plymouth Rock on Friday. Have them purposely do things on the 13th and use the number 13. Don't let him go through life being fearful of Friday, or the 13th, or black cats, etc. Teach the child that God is able to protect every day and that there are no accidents in the life of a Christian. Teach him Romans 8:28. Show him that everything works together for good if he loves God and stays in God's will. Hence, there are no accidents, there is no need for superstition, and the Christian can trust God for everything. So can the child!

There are many other fears that should be avoided or alleviated in the mind of a child. There are some justifiable fears that need to be placed in proper perspective. These are things which should be feared by the child. These fears should not, however, be exaggerated. Then there are things which the child should fear but which he should face. He should realize that the degree of courage is determined by the degree of fear. If there is no fear, there is no courage; simply recklessness. Over and over again the child should hear the words, "Use your own will. Let the will decide what you do. Let neither feelings nor fear control you."

Of course, one of the secrets to avoid, alleviate, and overcome fear, is to stay busy. Idle time is the time often spent in building imaginary enemies with imaginary ends and results. It is said that Sir Walter Scott dictated IVANHOE while he was in a painful condition. He kept his mind on his story and continued to write even though he was writhing in pain. Folks who watched him said that he would become so engrossed in the story that he would get up and pace from one side of the room to the other while dictating, obviously in pain but oblivious to it because he was busy. Think of the times our Lord came to troubled ones and said, "Fear not." May He speak those words to us and through us to our children that their lives may be free from unnecessary fears and full of courage to do right even when afraid to do so.

Chapter Fifteen

THE CHILD AT PLAY

The child at play is the child rehearsing for his future life. Actually he is using his powers to prepare himself for the activities of adult life. He is unconsciously instructing and educating himself to take his place in an adult society. The girl who plays house is rehearsing for her role as a wife and mother. The boy who plays store is rehearsing for his role as a merchant. The child who plays school is rehearsing for his role as a teacher. Such is also the case when a girl makes doll clothes and plays with her toy iron, dishes, pots and pans, broom, sweeper, etc. The boy is doing the same thing when he plays doctor, bus driver, truck driver, construction engineer, and the many other vocations for which a boy is rehearsing when he plays. Just as a little kitten plays with a ball or a leaf in the yard in order to prepare himself to catch mice, even so does the child play in preparation for adult life.

Just yesterday I saw my grandbaby for the first time. Becky, a new mother, was so proud as she showed Trina to me. My mind returned to Becky's childhood. She always loved dolls. Every Christmas she wanted some kind of a doll. As she cared for the doll she was preparing herself for this day, for today she has a "doll" of her own who will have a better mother because her mother played dolls as a little girl. It is not hard for those of us who are adults to see ourselves, our actions, and our behavior as in a mirror when we look at our children. They are preparing themselves to be like us as adults.

Because play is so important in the life of a child, the choice of what he plays should be directed by the parent as follows:

1. *Each child should be involved in playing games that develop his physical strength and coordination.* A child should have full opportunity to gratify his impulse to swing, run, jump, tumble, wrestle, swim, climb, etc. Of course, in our urbanized society this is not easy so parents in the city must work extra hard to see to it that children have opportunity to develop their abilities with physical exercises as they play.

I once saved the life of my sister because I had developed physical coordination while playing as a child. We were walking across the street together in South Bend, Indiana. A car was coming toward us which we could not see because of the sun. I saw it in time to jump. While I was in mid-air I grabbed her and pulled her away from the car so as the car hit her she was being pulled away. This made the impact much less. She was taken to the hospital, X-rayed, and found to be in good condition all because I had learned to jump in mid-air and relay the ball to second base, pass the basketball as I was in the air, etc. There is no doubt that the coordination I learned playing as a kid saved my sister's life. Many accidents in automobiles, boats, etc. occur because of people whose minds and muscles have not been properly coordinated through play in their youth. Often sudden emergencies paralyze a person's ability to respond because of a lack of proper coordination which could have been developed in childhood.

2. *The parent should insist the child play games that involve teamwork.* Such games would include less opportunity for individual excellence and more opportunity for the excellence of the group. Such group games are basketball, hockey, football, baseball, tennis (doubles), etc. These develop both

self-sacrifice and cooperation. They teach the child that he must work for others as others work for him. Especially is this important in the lives of children around the junior age; that is, 9, 10, 11 and 12. They are taught loyalty to the team, submission to authority and respect for the law. They are taught obedience to the leader, responsibility of the individual to his teammates, etc. Esprit de corps is developed and the child prepares himself to work with others in life which is so necessary. Here he learns to rejoice when others do well, he learns to be responsible for the sufferings of others, he learns fairness and justice, unselfishness and cooperation.

There are other ways the child can learn this. Being a member of the debating team, a dramatic club, or any other unit that requires cooperation and teamwork can accomplish the same purpose. This is very vital in proper rearing of children.

This is one reason for the rise of the hippie movement in our generation. It is one of the reasons for the increase in anarchy and the decrease in patriotism that is so prevalent in our generation.

3. *The parent should direct the child in playing things that prepare him for future life.* This has already been mentioned, but much stress should be given child's "playwork," so work can continue to be play and can become enjoyment to him instead of drudgery.

My three daughters—Becky, Linda and Cindy—have had play irons, cooking sets, dishes, pianos, etc. When Becky was a little girl she would ask for a "pian-la-la," which was the term she used for piano. She would bang away. Now she is an accomplished pianist. She was rehearsing before she ever owned a real piano.

Linda is now a cheerleader at our Christian high school. She is working as part of a team and she is being taught to work for the team as well as to cheer for others. This transferred in later years to adult life could give her an unselfishness that is so necessary to a full life.

Boys can have toy lawn mowers, hammers, saws, etc. that will prepare them for useful service as adults and teach them to enjoy work.

4. *The wise parent will not only teach the child to play, but will teach him to develop qualities found in the profession which he is imitating.* For example, when a boy plays soldier this presents the parent with a tremendous opportunity to teach him qualities about a soldier that he should possess, such as obedience, cleanliness, courage, chivalry, punctuality, good health habits, etc. The girl who plays nurse should be taught that all nurses should have compassion, promptness, good health, courtesy, kindness, and other qualities. Not only is the girl rehearsing for future activities, but she is rehearsing qualities that she should possess as an adult. When a little boy plays policeman, the wise parent will seize upon this opportunity to teach the boy that he should possess the conduct demanded for a good policeman—courage, neatness, politeness, etiquette, strength, helpfulness, chivalry, etc.

5. *The child should be encouraged to play things that are educational.* Games that teach life and the way to live it are desirable. When I was a boy I loved baseball and so I followed every baseball team in the country, both major league and minor league. I became acquainted with geography. I even learned mathematics as I would figure out batting averages. I knew where the New York Yankees were. I found on the map the locations of such cities as Cincinnati St. Louis, Detroit, Chicago, Philadelphia, Pittsburg, Cleveland, and Boston because I was interested in the athletic teams. In my play I was being educated.

6. *A child should be required to persevere as he plays.* A child who is building a model airplane should finish it. A child who is building a model car should be required to complete the project. The little girl who is playing like she is ironing must be required to iron all the doll clothes. The girl who washes the dishes must wash them well and finish the job before she quits. Hence, perseverance and determination are taught, and both are so vital in the training of a child to become a successful adult.

Cindy is left-handed. Because of this many tasks have not been easy for her. Especially was this true when she was a little girl. Over and over again I would teach her that though a task was hard she should finish it. Even in playing a game she learned perseverance. One of the reasons she is such a lovely girl now is because in many areas she played right as a little child.

7. *The parent should be what he ought to be and what he wishes his child to be.* Remember, the child plays what the parents do. A little boy asked his daddy for a quarter so he could play store. The daddy gave him only a penny whereupon the little boy replied, "Dad, it's store I want to play, not church."

The other day I was driving down the street and saw a little crowd of kids gathered around. A little girl was up on top of a box preaching. She was screaming, "You'd better get born again or you're going to hell when you die!" Then she took a little dog, raised her right hand and said, "In obedience to the command of our Lord and Master, and upon a public profession of your faith in Him, I baptize, you my _____ (I'm not sure whether it was a brother or sister), in the name of the Father, of the Son, and of the Holy Spirit, Amen." Then she took the dog and put it down in a little puddle of muddy water and raised it up. Do you know why she did that? She did it because she had seen her pastor do it through the years. Children play what we do. Let us be careful what we do. The child whose father smokes will no doubt have candy cigarettes. Remember, they play what they see us do.

8. *The parent should encourage the child to have a busy schedule of play.* This is especially helpful as the child grows to adolescence. It is so important that he have a busy schedule. It certainly helps in keeping him clean and pure. When I was a boy I would go to school, come home and throw my paper route, then hit the vacant lot. I would play baseball, basketball, or football according to the season until it was just too dark to see any more. Then I would go home, eat, and go to bed. Because I was busy and played games that were active, I am sure I kept out of a lot of trouble. Proper play is a powerful factor in making for purity. Without the legitimate vent of strenuous expression, the energy of passion in developing finds vent in bad forms of expression.

9. *The parent should set times of play.* In others words, he should schedule playtimes. This is teaching the child through games to rehearse for life by having a schedule and being disciplined.

J. P. Holland said, "Play is a sacred thing, a divine ordinance for developing in the child harmonious and healthy organism and preparing the organism for the commencement of the work of life." Because of this, play should be encouraged and directed by the parent. Care should be taken to disallow any games that lead to vices. I have always outlawed the use of dice in the playing of a game. Sometimes this has been a problem. However, in playing a game like Monopoly we have used a spinner with numbers from one to twelve. This is just as acceptable as dice and does not familiarize the children with something that has been so long associated with gambling. I have also led the children not to play games that are played with cards so they would not become accustomed to playing cards. The question comes up often concerning a child's playing with guns. I have always allowed my children to play with guns. I have taught them the proper use of guns and have discouraged their pointing them at people and carelessly shooting. I have explained that a gun is for protection, for hunting, etc. Of course, each parent will have to use his own discretion and God-given wisdom as he makes such arbitrary decisions.

Chapter Sixteen

THE CHILD AND HIS CHURCH

In Luke 4:16 we read, *"And He came to Nazareth, where He had been brought up: and, as His custom was, He went into the synagogue on the sabbath day, and stood up for to read."* If the synagogue had such an important part in the life of Jesus, the Son of God, how much more do our children need the New Testament church! The church is the family's best friend and its confines should be the child's second home.

1. *The child should be taken to church very soon after birth.* No one really knows when the first influences are made on the life of a child and when the first impressions reach his little mind. I well recall that when Becky was born I went to the hospital with a big Scofield Reference Bible, stood in front of the window, looked in at her little face, waved the Bible back and forth, and hollered, "Becky, this is the Bible. The Bible is the Word of God." She was not impressed, but I wanted her first impression to concern spiritual matters.

The first night she was home from the hospital I walked her much of the night. As I did so I told her about Adam and Eve, the fall of man, Abraham and Isaac, Isaac and Rebekah, Jacob and Esau, Noah, Ham, Shem, Japheth, Moses, David, Daniel, Shadrach, Meshach, Abednego, the virgin birth, the sinless life, the vicarious death, the bodily resurrection, the second coming, the rapture, the judgment seat, the marriage of the Lamb, the millennium, the Great White Throne, Heaven and Hell. I then told her the plan of salvation from front to back. She was only a few days old. She did not seem very impressed, but I wanted her to know everything she should know about the Bible. Periodically I told her how to be saved until she was old enough to know and receive Christ for herself.

When Becky was six days old I took her to the church nursery. When David was ten days old he was in the nursery. When Linda was nine days old she was in the nursery. When Cindy was a week and a half she was in the nursery. It is very important that a child be taken to church at the earliest time possible. Of course, this means that the church nursery should be one of the finest, cleanest and best equipped rooms in the entire church. It should be cheerful, spotlessly clean, and staffed with the finest and most careful workers. The other day I was walking by our church nursery and saw this little sign over the cribs: "We shall not all sleep, but we shall all be changed." Of course, this was taken from the Apostle Paul and had nothing to do with the church nursery, but it simply points out the fact that someone cares for the children, and there is a delight even in the nursery of the church. Recently the superintendent of our four nursery suites gave each little child a bib on which was printed, "I LOVE MY PREACHER!"

2. *The child should be reared in the right kind of a church.* By all means, the parent should not allow his child to attend a modernistic church. Every child has a God-given right to grow up in a church that believes the Bible is the Word of God, the deity of Christ, His miracles, His virgin birth, His bodily resurrection, the truth of Heaven and Hell, and the fundamental Bible doctrines. Parents should see to it that their children are not under the influence of a modernistic preacher who denies the Bible and its Christ.

The idea of "going to the church of your choice" is

certainly contrary to the teachings of the Word of God. We should go to the church of His choice.

Another dangerous trend is that of going to the church that is nearest. No one does this in other areas of life. No one goes to the grocery store because it is the nearest one. No man goes to the barber shop because it is the closest one. We choose the places to which we feel we ought to go, and certainly the right kind of church is necessary for rearing the right kind of child.

3. *The child should be taught faithfulness to all the services of the church.* This is very, very important. The child should get the idea that when the doors of the church are open he should be there. He should never miss Sunday school, morning preaching, Sunday evening youth meetings, Sunday evening preaching service, or the Wednesday evening service. One of the things my mother impressed upon my little heart when I was a boy that I have never fogotten is the fact that when the church doors are open we are supposed to be there.

4. *The child should build his entire life around the local church.* Because of this the church must intensify its program for the child as he grows older. Before a baby is born he is completely dependent upon his mother. He can eat only when his mother eats. He can go only where his mother goes. At birth, when the cord is cut, a severance begins that is gradual but definite. This severance ends when the child leaves home to go off to college, to the service, or to establish his own home by marriage. During the growing up years as this severance continues and the child finds himself spending more and more time away from the home, the church should pick up the void that is left. This is why at the First Baptist Church of Hammond we increase the activities offered to the child with the passing of the years. We

figure that a beginner child (ages 4 and 5) is 90% tied to his parents. Consequently, we do not offer a great deal in extracurricular activities for the beginner child. We feel that the primary child (ages 6 and 7) is perhaps 75% tied to his parents, so we increase the extra-curricular activities for him.

As the child approaches the junior age he continues to spend more and more time away from his parents. He is now busy in school. He is the age for Boy Scouts, Little League baseball, etc. Consequently, we surmise that perhaps he needs 50% of his time filled. Hence, the church intensifies its program. As he becomes a junior high school student, perhaps he is 75% severed from his parents. The church must then provide even more activities for the junior highers.

When he enrolls in high school he is coming toward the last steps of preparing himself for his own life. He is gone from home more, so he needs more extra-curricular activities at the church. Because of this the church should multiply its efforts to provide for the total need of the teenager.

At the First Baptist Church of Hammond we have a weekly activity for the young people. This is church-wide and is sponsored by the church and directed by a youth director. This activity is sometimes social and sometimes strictly spiritual. One week a month services are conducted by our youth at the Pacific Garden Rescue Mission in Chicago. Sometimes there is a youth rally, sometimes a weiner roast, sometimes a party, at other times a Christian movie, but there is something every week.

Then also, each Saturday evening our teenagers meet to go to soul winning. An average of 125 teenagers meet on their own and go out to win others to Jesus Christ.

We choose the finest of workers to work with the teenagers, especially the high schoolers. We have singing groups of all sizes and types for them. There is a large high school choir (also a junior high choir). This high school choir is well drilled, and the musical program of the church as far as the young people are concerned far exceeds that of the school system. The child should definitely be taught there is nothing at the church done that is second-rate. It is always first-rate. Everything is done properly.

Mark Twain once said, "When a child becomes a teenager he should be placed in a box with a hole just large enough so he can breathe. When he gets to be seventeen, plug up the hole." This need not be so if the child is faithful to the activities of the church.

Parents should see to it that the child is in every activity. For example, in the First Baptist Church of Hammond the high schooler should go soul winning, go to the weekly youth activity, attend the youth choir, and join in all the Sunday school parties, etc. The entire void that is left as a child approaches the leaving of his parents should be filled by the church. Especially is this true as the public schools become more worldly and as the temptations of the world become greater.

5. *The child should be taught to give church activities preference over school activities.* This is not to say that school is unimportant. Quite to the contrary! The school is important, but not as important as the New Testament church. The wise parent will see that his children study and that they obey the school teacher and cooperate in every right endeavor at school as long as these endeavors do not conflict with the church activities. For example, if there is a school activity on Wednesday night, the child should go to prayer meeting. He should get the idea that Matthew 6:33 is true when our Lord admonishes us, *"But seek ye first the kingdom of God, and His righteousness."*

6. *The parent who is wise will build in his child a confidence in his pastor.* This is so important!

I am thinking now of a family in our church. They are good people. They are faithful people, but they developed a little habit of complaining about the pastor. They would drop little bits of criticism around the supper table. They did not mean to be critical and certainly not hurtful, but the children soaked it up until they began to lose confidence in the pastor. The girl became a teenager. She was drifting away from God and needed her pastor desperately; in fact, I was the only person who could have helped her. (This was generally agreed.) She had, however, heard her parents criticize the pastor so much that she would not come to him for counsel. The criticisms were not of a serious nature and the truth is, the parents are for the pastor and behind his program. They simply would speak carelessly that his sermons were too long, the invitation song was sung too fast, his tie was too loud, etc. Though they meant nothing by it, the daughter thought they did, and her life has been ruined because the parents did not build her confidence in the pastor.

The wise parent will see to it that the child develops a close relationship with the pastor. The pastor should become in every sense his hero! When the parents can see this is true, they can build the pastor up in the eyes of the children, admonish them to obey him, and do what he says. In so doing, they are guaranteeing that the child will come to the pastor when a need arises. How vital and important this is! To be sure, the pastor is not perfect, and the parents should not tell the child that he is. Neither should the parent dwell on his imperfections, but rather, strengthen the relationship of the child with the pastor.

After every public service parents bring their

children to my study. If the child's grades are bad, they bring him to me for counsel. If there is a problem of disobedience, they bring him to me for conversation. A sweet relationship exists between the pastor and the children which enables the pastor to be able to help them when they have special need of help.

7. *The child should be taught to behave properly at church.* There is an important point to be mentioned here. Far too many children are taught to behave at church because "it is the Lord's house." We imply to the child that the Lord lives in the church building and that we come by to see Him on Sunday. This is an improper motive for proper behavior. The church building is the house of God simply by ownership. He does not live in the church building any more than He does in the home, but the church is a place dedicated to the teaching of His word and the fellowshipping of His people. If for no other reason, the child should certainly be taught that the equipment at church is paid for from God's money, and he should not damage the songbooks, the pews, or any other property owned by the church. Both pastor and parent should see that the child behaves properly at church. This should be especially true in the teenage years. The teenager needs to hear what the man of God says. He also needs to learn to be decent and orderly in public gatherings, especially when they are conducted in the house built with God's money.

8. *The child should be taught to give tithes and offerings to the church.* This should be done at the earliest age. When a child makes his first dime he should be taught that one penny of it belongs to God and that if he gives an offering, it should be more than the one penny. This will enable the child to start a practice which will keep him from ever robbing

God.

One of the finest things that ever happened to me was that I grew up close to churches. When I was six years of age we lived two houses from the church. My mother cleaned the church building every week for $2 a week. I went with her and stayed around the church building. When I was thirteen we moved across the street from our church. I was always there. I was more faithful to the church than was the church mouse. It was my second home. All of my life and activities were centered around a fundamental, Bible-preaching church. The wise parent will see to it that his child does likewise.

Chapter Seventeen

KEEPING THE CHILD PURE

Satan has pointed every weapon in his arsenal at our young people. Promiscuous petting, Hollywood movies, secular magazines, the new morality, ludeness in dress, television, popular songs, and the permissive society have all joined hands to try to corrupt the morals of our youth. If a child reaches the marriage altar retaining his purity in our generation, it certainly will be on purpose and not by accident. It will be the result of prayer, training, and discipline as administered by loving parents. This chapter is dedicated to helping us to rear clean, chaste, and moral young people.

1. *The child should attend a fundamental church that takes a stand against the permissive society, indecent dress, improper exposure of the body, and unwise association between the sexes.* He should hear a man of God thunder against sin and for righteousness. He should be taught the "thou shalt nots" of the Bible. He should get the idea from early childhood that he is to keep his body pure and clean and save it for the one God has for him.

He should be taught the Scriptures which deal with virtue and chastity. There is absolutely no substitute for a child growing up at the feet of a prophet of God, a man who rains wrath upon evil and warns men of evil deeds.

2. *The wise parent will have definite rules about a boy and girl not being in a car alone together.* Becky is now married. She was never allowed to be alone in a car with a boy. More sin is committed in

automobiles than in motel rooms and red-light districts. The wise parent will never say such things as "I trust my daughter." The truth is he should not even trust himself in a circumstance that would lead to wrong. The Apostle Paul was always conscious of the possibility of his turning back. He warned the Galatian church if he himself returned and preached any gospel other than the one they had heard, he should be accursed. The child who does not spend hours and hours alone with a member of the opposite sex in a car certainly has not missed anything that he shouldn't miss.

3. *A child should obey strict rules concerning his hours out of the house.* Eleven o'clock has always been curfew at our house, and it is late enough for any child or teenager to be out. When Becky and her fiancé, Tim, were planning their wedding with me in my office, we were discussing the time of the wedding. Tim suggested a certain hour and Becky looked at him with a startled expression and said, "Tim, we can't have it that late; we couldn't get in by eleven!" All those years of being in by eleven had impressed her and subconsciously she felt she should be in by eleven o'clock even on her wedding night.

Not only should these rules be set, but they should be rigidly enforced. When I was a boy I was always in by eleven, but at the age of 17 one night I was with the wrong crowd and I stayed out until after one o'clock. At one o'clock the wine bottle was passed around in the car. There were six of us present. Five took a drink. The bottle was in my hand and I lifted it to my mouth when suddenly conviction like an arrow pierced my heart. I threw the bottle down and spilled it on the floor of the car and shouted, "TAKE ME HOME!" They laughed and made fun, but they took me home. When I got home I saw a beautiful sight. My mother was kneeling in front of the old wood stove praying for me. She was praying something like this: "Dear Lord, bless Jack. Keep him pure, keep him clean. He has always been a good boy. You know, dear Lord, I have had to be both a mother and father to Jack. I have done my best. Please take care of him and help him to be a good boy."

I then said, "Mama."

She looked up and jumped into my arms and said, "Son, I knew you wouldn't do anything wrong." That was the last time I ever got home late. Let us teach our boys and girls to have strict hours.

4. *The parent should teach the child the sanctity of the body.* Girls should be taught that their bodies are very sacred and should be treated as such. A boy should be taught of the sanctity of his own body and of how sacred is the body of little girls. Children should be reminded that the body is the temple of the Holy Spirit. Each child should be taught to keep his own body dedicated and pure and to observe the sanctity of the opposite sex.

5. *The child should be taught to be disciplined in his eating habits.* This may seem strange in a chapter on purity, but children who have no restraint in the feeding of their bodies will likely have little or no restraint in resisting other temptations that come to the body. If leaving off stimulating food such as sauces, highly seasoned food, and other foods hard to digest does nothing else, it at least teaches the child to say "no" to the appetites of the body. This discipline can be transferred to the temptation of immorality and misbehavior toward the opposite sex. One discipline helps another.

6. *Proper clothing should be worn.* Tight clothing should be discouraged. Clothing that needlessly irritates the body should not be worn. Clothing that exposes too much of the body should be avoided.

7. *The child should have the proper physical*

exercise. Active, muscular exercise utilizes a vital force that is a powerful moral factor. It is best that a child have plenty of physical exercise.

8. *The parent should see to it that the child is very busy.* Somebody has said that the only men free from bad habits were those whose paths kept them so everlastingly busy that they never had any time to go loafing. The parent should help create hobbies that will tend to fill the idle hours as well as keep boys and girls apart much of the time. Seize every opportunity to use a child's interests toward a proper hobby.

Along this line it is wise for a child not to develop hobbies that are quiet and cause him to be alone. Too many hours of listening to stereo music is not good. Too many hours of playing alone is not good. Hours spent behind locked doors are dangerous. Outdoor games are better than indoor games. Active games are better than quiet games. Group games are better than games played alone.

9. *The child should not be allowed to attend Hollywood movies or read questionable literature.* Plenty of good literature should be provided, especially novels of adventure, heroic action, etc.

10. *When a child reaches the teen years he should be challenged by his parents to set a goal of staying pure until he gives himself to the one of God's choice.* This should be stressed over and over again so that he will work and point toward such a goal. It should be one of the biggest goals in his life and should be constantly kept before him.

11. *The child should never be allowed to see his parents unclothed.* Modern psychologists and counselors seem to think they know more than God along this line. The simple truth is that the Lord frowns on children being able to see the body of the parent. Such things as bathing together, undressing

together, etc. should be taboo! It is unscriptural.

12. *Little boys should play with little boys and little girls with little girls.* Becky, Linda, and Cindy have never been allowed to play with little boys, and David has never been allowed to play with little girls. So many of our children have drifted toward homosexuality because of boys developing feminine tendencies and girls developing masculine tendencies.

13. *The child should never be allowed to be alone unclothed or scantily clothed.* After bathing he should be required to clothe himself completely. This eliminates presenting unnecessary opportunities for a child fondling his own body or becoming overly interested in himself and his body.

14. *A girl should do girl's work and a boy should do boy's work.* In an effort to make ladies of girls and men of boys the parent should see to it that the girl does not mow the yard, prune the trees, chop the garden, etc. These are boys' tasks. The boys should not wash the dishes, iron, etc. These are girls' tasks. The boy should mow the yard, clean the garage, clean the basement, do repair work around the house, etc., and by all means he should be taught to sweat. This is vital, not only in making him normal, but also in keeping him pure.

15. *The mother should counsel with the daughter and the father with the son.* In some cases the order may have to be reversed because of parents being unwilling to cooperate, but children should be taught as they grow older about reproduction, etc. All writers on the subject of sexual immorality agree that it is largely due to ignorance. Because this is true, this does not give the school teacher a license to train someone else's child about such delicate and sacred subjects. There comes a time in the life of a young lady when she needs to have a talk with her mother. It may be explained to her that for long months she

was a part of her mother's life and after long days of pain, suffering, and discomfort, she actually came from her mother's body. With tender words, nothing but the holiest feelings can be aroused from such a conversation. Children, should be taught to talk on these subjects with no one but their mothers and fathers. It should be explained that this is too sacred a field to discuss with others and that God has made this so sacred that the discussion should be within the family circle.

A girl has a right to instruction concerning the hygiene of menstruation, the function and sacredness of motherhood, and care of infants. The time when this should be taught is up to the individual mother, but it should always be done very privately, sweetly, tenderly, and with prayerful and godly atmosphere.

Boys and girls should be taught of proper hygiene. They should be warned about venereal diseases and should in general be instructed by those who love them most and those whom God gave them to instruct them concerning life.

Stress should be given to the fact that no joke should ever be told about something so sacred. Girls should be taught to shrink from every touch and to resent any approach to familiarity upon the part of a boy. Again, let it be emphasized that the parent should decide when these subjects are approached. They alone should teach them. When young people decide to marry, the wise parent will have a long talk with the young person giving him proper books to read and advising him to seek medical advice concerning marriage, love, reproduction, etc. Let there be much charity given as we think of when and how the aforementioned should be done, but let us leave it to the parents and not shove the responsibility off to some public school teacher whom we hardly know, if at all. The modern sex education program in our public schools is certainly unwise, unscriptural, and oftentimes immoral. Let us keep something so sacred in the confines of the family circle or at best within the confines of the pastor, doctor, and parents.

Chapter Eighteen

TEACHING RESPECT AND HONOR
FOR PARENTS

It is very interesting to note the importance that God places on children respecting and honoring parents. The fifth through the tenth of the Ten Commandments deal with man's relationship to his fellowman. The first of these says, *"Honour thy father and thy mother: that thy days may be long upon the land which the Lord thy God giveth thee."* (Exodus 20:12) This same commandment is repeated in the New Testament in Ephesians 6:1-3, *"Children, obey your parents in the Lord: for this is right. Honour thy father and mother; which is the first commandment with promise; That it may be well with thee, and thou mayest live long on the earth."*

Under the Old Testament law the son who was rebellious against his parents was stoned for this rebellion. Deuteronomy 21:18-21, *"If a man have a stubborn and rebellious son, which will not obey the voice of his father, or the voice of his mother, and that, when they have chastened him, will not hearken unto them: Then shall his father and his mother lay hold on him, and bring him out unto the elders of his city, and unto the gate of his place; And they shall say unto the elders of his city, This our son is stubborn and rebellious, he will not obey our voice; he is a glutton, and a drunkard. And all the men of his city shall stone him with stones, that he die: so shall thou put evil away from among you; and all Israel shall hear, and fear."*

This is not to say that same thing should be done in this dispensation. It is, however, important to stress

the fact that God is opposed to rebellion and
disobedience toward one's parents. Notice again in
Exodus 20:12 the last portion says, *"that thy days
may be long upon the land which the Lord thy God
giveth thee."* God promises a long life to the
individual who is obedient to his father and mother.
No doubt this is because the kind of life which is a
life of obedience will involve self-discipline and
restraint that would enable one to have a long life and
good health. Then too, there is the simple promise
from God that He will give us longer life if we will
obey our parents. Hence, the mother and father who
teach the child strict obedience and respect are not
only giving him a happier life but a longer life. It is
then imperative, for a child to have the fullest life
possible, he should be taught from infancy to respect
and honor his mother and father. How can this be
done?

1. *Require strict obedience.* This obedience should
always be immediate, instant, without question or
argument. What the father says do, the son does. He
does it well, he does it immediately, and he does it
without argument. The parents allow no exceptions
to the rule. Hence, obedience is the law of the land
and the child should not deem it necessary to have an
explanation for the orders he has received from his
parents. Many unconverted psychologists say that the
parents should always take time to explain to the
child why he should do certain things and that
parents should never command a child to do
something without the child knowing the reason.
Nothing could be further from the truth! The parents
should not have to convince the child the logic
behind their orders. This same thing transferred into
adult life will bring anarchy to a society. The
Scriptures are very plain concerning obedience.
Colossians 3:20, *"Children, obey your parents in all*

things: for this is well pleasing unto the Lord."
Ephesians 6:1, *"Children, obey your parents in the Lord: for this is right."* Obedience is the foundation for all character. It is the foundation for the home. It is the foundation for a school. It is the foundation for a country. It is the foundation for a society. It is absolutely necessary for law and order to prevail.

2. *Proper respect for parents includes their being addressed properly.* The modern idea of calling fathers and mothers by their first names certainly is promoting a familiarity that will not lead to respect, obedience, or honor. Many have the idea that the father should be just a big brother or a buddy to the child and that the mother should act as a pal or big sister to the girl. The offices of mother and father should demand more respect than that! My father was not a Christian, in fact, he was a drunkard. My home was broken; yet I always called him "Daddy." I would never have spoken to him as "Willis" or "Athey." This same holds true in any position of authority. The pastor should not be called by his first name. Many youth workers are unwise in allowing teenagers to call them by their first names. This, of course, is done many times with proper motives and it is caused by sincere, genuine humility on the part of the worker, but it does not teach the child proper respect for authority.

The other day I was walking down the alley behind our church. A little boy about six years of age said, "Hi, Jack." I turned, picked him up by the collar, held him up to where our noses touched, and I said, "What did you call me?"

He said, "Br-br-br-br-other Hyles."

I said, "Let it always be so."

Now Brother Hyles is nobody, but the job of Pastor of First Baptist Church of Hammond is something and that position should be respected.

Likewise, the titles parent, mother, and father are important ones and the children should always address their parents with proper titles. Some children call their father "Dad," while others say, "Daddy," "Papa," or "Father." These are all acceptable. My children have all called me "Dad." The title given to the mother should be "Mom," "Mama," "Mother," or "Mommy." All of these are likewise acceptable.

3. *In order for the child to respect his parents properly he should never see them unclothed.* He should respect the person of mother and father. Leviticus 18:7, *"The nakedness of thy father, or the nakedness of thy mother, shalt thou not uncover: she is thy mother; thou shalt not uncover her nakedness."*

The awful sin that Ham committed was that of seeing his father unclothed. Genesis 9:20-27, *"And Noah began to be an husbandman, and he planted a vineyard: And he drank of the wine, and was drunken; and he was uncovered within his tent. And Ham, the father of Canaan, saw the nakedness of his father, and told his two brethren without. And Shem and Japheth took a garment, and laid it upon both their shoulders, and went backward, and covered the nakedness of their father; and their faces were backward, and they saw not their father's nakedness. And Noah awoke from his wine, and knew what his younger son had done unto him. And he said, Cursed be Canaan; a servant of servants shall he be unto his brethren. And he said, Blessed be the Lord God of Shem; and Canaan shall be his servant. God shall enlarge Japheth, and he shall dwell in the tents of Shem; and Canaan shall be his servant."* Noah, his father, was drunk. Ham saw his nakedness and a curse was placed upon his son, Canaan, for this.

Hence, parents should be clothed properly in the presence of their children. This tends to create reverence for the person of the parent. Modern psychologists and counselors in using the wisdom of man present their unscriptural ideas about preparing the child for adulthood by allowing him to see the nude bodies of his parents.

4. *Children should always address their parents with "Yes, sir," "No, sir," "Yes, ma'am," and "No, ma'am."* This is not because a child is a slave and the mother and dad are tyrants. It is because the mother and dad represent God and fill an important office. This is the reason the enlisted man in the army says, "Yes, sir" to the officer. It is not because the officer is better than the enlisted man; it is because he fills a position of authority. This position should be respected by the use of "Yes, sir." It is wise for this "Yes, sir," "No, sir," "Yes, ma'am" and "No, ma'am" to be transferred to every area of authority and to all adults.

5. *The child should show respect for his parents by preferring them.* When going through the door the child should step back and allow the parent to go first. Dad should have the best seat; Mom should have the most comfortable place on the sofa, and the children should always prefer the mother and father. This is teaching the child respect for age, authority, position, and also consideration for others. Of course, this should not be done so the parent can have "the biggest end of the stick." It is not done because of the selfishness of the parent; it is done because of the wisdom of the parent who wants to teach the child to be unselfish. If unselfishness is developed in early childhood, it must be done toward the parents and other children since the young child has so few contacts outside his own home. The child who is selfish at home will not suddenly develop unselfishness outside the home. If he is to be unselfish when he goes to school, when he plays, etc.,

he must be unselfish during his early years while he is most of the time confined with his parents.

6. *The child should be taught that proper respect for his parents includes caring for them and providing them financial support when they are older.* As is pointed out in other chapters children should be trained during their early years to support their mom and dad during their latter years. It is alarming how many parents are dumped on the government by ungrateful children who were reared in the homes of unwise parents.

The parents who teach their children to respect and honor them are not being selfish. They are guaranteeing their child longer life, a richer and fuller life, and a life that is built around the needs of others. They are also guaranteeing themselves a happier and more prosperous old age.

Chapter Nineteen

THE BIBLE AND PRAYER
IN A CHILD'S LIFE

Prayer and Bible study in the life of a child should be just as normal as playing, eating, sleeping, and talking. In order to insure this, both should have a vital part in the child's life from infancy. Prayer should be as natural as conversation and Bible reading should be as natural as reading the newspaper. It should be considered routine and acceptable so as to include God in every decision of the family as well as in every conversation and activity.

1. *There should be prayer at mealtime.* A simple earnest prayer of thanksgiving for the food and of asking God's blessings on the food should be offered before each meal. Our Lord did this in Luke 24:30 and 31, *"And it came to pass, as He sat at meat with them, He took bread, and blessed it, and brake, and gave to them. And their eyes were opened, and they knew Him; and He vanished out of their sight."*

The Apostle Paul in writing to young Timothy reminded him that this should be done. I Timothy 4:1-5, *"Now the Spirit speaketh expressly, that in the latter times some shall depart from the faith, giving heed to seducing spirits, and doctrines of devils; Speaking lies in hypocrisy; having their conscience seared with a hot iron; Forbidding to marry, and commanding to abstain from meats, which God hath created to be received with thanksgiving of them which believe and know the truth. For every creature of God is good, and nothing to be refused, if it be received with thanksgiving: For it is sanctified by the word of God and prayer."*

Then Paul himself after a time of fasting blessed the food that he ate in Acts 27:33-37, *"And while the day was coming on, Paul besought them all to take meat, saying, This day is the fourteenth day that ye have tarried and continued fasting, having taken nothing. Wherefore I pray you to take some meat: for this is for your health: for there shall not an hair fall from the head of any of you. And when he had thus spoken, he took bread, and gave thanks to God in presence of them all: and when he had broken it, he began to eat. Then were they all of good cheer, and they also took some meat. And we were in all in the ship two hundred threescore and sixteen souls."*

When prayer is said at mealtime the children learn to be grateful for the food. It is a simple teaching of the Scripture that the food will better nourish the body of the child if it is received with thanksgiving.

2.   *The Bible should be taught to the children.* Especially is this true when the children are little. They should learn the basic Bible stories such as "The Prodigal Son," "Sampson," "David and Goliath," "Baby Moses," "Noah and the Ark," "Daniel and the Lion's Den," "Shadrach, Meshach, and Abednego in the Fiery Furnace," "The Battle of Jericho," etc. These stories as well as other parts of the Word of God may be taught in the family circle or in private sessions with the child. My mother used to teach me the Bible with just the two of us alone. Ah, how she could make the stories of the Bible live to me, and how they helped in forming the principles by which I have tried to live!

There are some good Bible story books that the parents could use to teach to the child. One of the best of these is Egermeier's. Another is Hurlbut's. Sunday school is wonderful and Vacation Bible School is good, but neither of these can take the place of the

Bible being taught to the children at home, especially in the early years.

3. *The children should memorize the Bible!* This can be done as a family group while their little minds are vital and tender. By the time Cindy was seven she could quote Psalms 1, 8, 19, 23, 95, 100, much of 103, 117, 121, and 126; I Corinthians 13; much of Romans 8; and many other passages in the Bible. Start when a child is very young and memorize the Scripture.

II Timothy 3:15 and 16, *"And that from a child thou hast known the holy scriptures, which are able to make thee wise unto salvation through faith which is in Christ Jesus. All scripture is given by inspiration of God, and is profitable for doctrine, for reproof, for correction, for instruction in righteousness."*

You will note that from a child Timothy had been taught the Scriptures by his mother and grandmother. The word "child" here means "very young child." These are the years when it is easier for the child to learn and memorize. These tender and impressive years should be seized upon by the parents.

4. *The parents should pray with the child when special needs arise.* The child should be taught to bring everything to God in prayer.

When Becky was a little girl she had a tooth that was about ready to be pulled. I tried and tried and tried but simply could not get a good enough hold on the tooth to make it come out. Becky looked up and said, "Daddy, let's ask Jesus to help you pull it the next time you try." So we bowed our heads and asked God to help us pull the tooth. The next time the tooth came out.

When Linda was a little girl she was very sick. Every night I would slip into her room, have a prayer with her for God's healing mercies to be upon her body. These special prayers can be offered in a family group prayer time. They can also be offered as the parent and child pray alone together. The main idea is for the child to get the idea that God is interested in every phase of his life. There is nothing in the life of the child that is unimportant to God and the child should nave nothing in his life that he cannot bring to God in prayer.

When Cindy was younger she was afraid of storms. Many times we have bowed our heads and asked God to watch over us through the storm and give us peace and assurance of safety.

When David was a little fellow he sucked his thumb. I made this a matter of prayer and the two of us many times asked God to help David about his thumbsucking, and God did.

5. *The child should be taught to have a private devotion daily.* This devotional time should probably be in the morning before the day begins. Great Christians have traditionally started the day with God. Moody began the day in early prayer. John Wesley rose to pray at four o'clock every morning. He prayed for two hours. Some said to him that they were too busy to pray for two hours a day. He replied that he was too busy not to pray two hours a day. Other great Christians such as Payson, Fletcher, Judson, David Brainerd, and Spurgeon have testified that they met God in the morning times. Here is the opportunity for the boy or girl to ask God for strength for the day, for power to resist temptation, for wisdom to make the right decisions and for leadership in all he does.

6. *Children should always say bedtime prayers.* In the early years perhaps the child would repeat the same prayer each night, but as soon as possible he should say his own prayer.

When I was a little fellow my mother taught me to pray this prayer, "Now I lay me down to sleep, I pray the Lord my soul to keep; If I should die before I wake, I pray the Lord my soul to take. Bless Mommy, Daddy, Earlyne (my sister), Jack, and everybody. Make me a good little boy. Amen." I said this prayer every night as a child.

When I became nine years of age I came to my mother one day and said, "Mother, I think I'm old enough now to make up my own prayer and quit saying that baby prayer." Mother began to weep a little bit and so I bowed my head and said again, "Now I lay me down to sleep, I pray the Lord my soul to keep; If I should die before I wake, I pray the Lord my soul to take. Bless Mommy, Daddy, Earlyne, Jack, and everybody. Make me a good little boy. Amen."

When I became thirteen years of age I realized I was a teenager. One night I said to Mother, "Now listen, Mom. I'm a teenager and teenagers don't say silly little prayers like 'Now I lay me down to sleep.'" Mother looked at me and said, with tears in her eyes, "Of course, son," and as her lips began to quiver and tears rolled down her cheeks, I said, "Now I lay me down to sleep, I pray the Lord my soul to keep; If I should die before I wake, I pray the Lord my soul to take. Bless Mommy, Daddy, Earlyne, Jack, and everybody. Make me a good little boy. Amen."

When I was seventeen I had my first date. When I got in from my first date I said to mother, "Now look, Mom! I'm seventeen and I'm going with the girls now. I am too old to say, 'Now I lay me down to sleep.'" Again she agreed and again the tears came. When I saw the tears I said, "Now I lay me down to sleep, I pray the Lord my soul to keep; If I should die before I wake, I pray the Lord my soul to take. Bless Mommy, Daddy, Earlyne, Jack, and everybody. Make me a good little boy. Amen."

Believe it or not, when I went in the army in World

War II I was still saying, "Now I lay me down to
sleep." I was away in service for awhile until I got my
first furlough. When I came home I found Mother had
prepared my favorite food. Ah, it was so good to be
home and she was so glad to see her only son! We ate,
talked about old times, started to catch up on our
conversation, and soon it was bedtime. I laid down
and soon was off to sleep, only to be awakened by
some sniffling. I looked up and there stood my
mother in her old-fashioned nightgown looking down
toward my bed. The lights were out but the moon
was bright and my mother was silhoutted in the door
of my room. I looked up and said, "Mother, what's
wrong?"

Her little independent spirit prompted her to say,
"Can't a body have a cold?" I turned over and went
back to sleep. Again I was awakened by some
sobbing. I looked up and there was my mother still
standing in the doorway. She seemed to be crying. I
asked, "Mother, what's wrong? Are you crying?"

She replied, "Did you ever hear of sinus trouble?"
I turned over and went back to sleep.

A few minutes later I was awakened for the third
time. I looked up and saw my mother weeping. I
asked her what the trouble was. She had a
handkerchief in her hand and she was twisting it. She
said, "Son, would you . . . uh . . . just one more
time . . . . er . . . uh . . ."

I looked up and said, "Mommy, pray me." Then I
said, "Now I lay me down to sleep, I pray the Lord
my soul to keep; If I should die before I wake, I pray
the Lord my soul to take. Bless Mommy, Daddy,
Earlyne, Jack, and everybody. Make me a good little
boy. Amen."

I am so grateful that my mother taught me to pray.
I am not sure that it is wise for a person to pray the
baby prayer when he is in the army, but the principle

is there just the same. The wise parent will teach his child to pray about everything.

As the child grows in Bible knowledge and in the prayer life, the parent should watch carefully for any conditions that may point to the child's readiness for salvation. The Bible is very plain in teaching that it is the parent's job to win the children to Christ. Joshua guaranteed the salvation of his children in Joshua 24:15. *"And if it seem evil unto you to serve the Lord, choose you this day whom ye will serve; whether the gods which your fathers served that were on the other side of the flood, or the gods of the Amorites, in whose land ye dwell: but as for me and my house, we will serve the Lord."*

The Philippian jailor saw his children converted immediately upon his salvation, for the Apostle Paul guaranteed him that if he would get converted, he could win his children. Acts 16:33 and 34, *"And he took them the same hour of the night, and washed their stripes; and was baptized, he and all his, straightway. And when he had brought them into his house, he set meat before them, and rejoiced, believing in God with all his house."*

When the child shows signs of conviction the parent should explain the plan of salvation to him very carefully, and as soon as the parent has the assurance that the child is ready, he should lead him to Christ. Then it seems wise for the parent to contact the pastor, taking the child in for a conference so the pastor may give counsel and lend his wisdom to the course of action that should be taken. The if both pastor and parent are satisfied that the salvation is genuine, they should encourage the child to be baptized and to join the church.

With the church and the parents working together children can be taught that prayer and Bible study are as much a part of life as breathing. If children never cease to feel this way, they can become great Christians with a good knowledge of the Bible and with a confidence that God hears and answers their prayers and is concerned about every detail of their lives.

Chapter Twenty

HOW TO MAKE A LADY OUT OF A GIRL

The women's liberation notwithstanding most men still want someone ladylike and feminine for a wife. To be sure, all good Christian men want submissive, feminine, ladylike, and godly wives. Yet, we live in a society which wants to homogenize the sexes. The boys wear long hair and the girls wear short hair. The boys wear make-up and the girls wear blue jeans. The boys wear flowered shirts while the girls wear work shirts. The fad is for the boys to be feminine and the girls to be masculine. Consequently, if parents rear a girl to be ladylike, they will be swimming upstream, going against the grain, and climbing uphill, but it can be done. If it is done, however, it will be on purpose and some of the following suggestions must be used in order to make a lady out of a girl.

1. *Dress her like a girl.* Let her have long hair. Let her wear lace and ribbons. Do not let her wear that which pertaineth to a man. Deuteronomy 22:5 says, *"The woman shall not wear that which pertaineth unto a man, neither shall a man put on a woman's garment: for all that do so are abomination unto the Lord thy God."* The parent who wants to make a young lady of a daughter should see to it that she does not wear revealing clothes, but that she dresses modestly. I Timothy 2:9 and 10 says, *"In like manner also, that women adorn themselves in modest apparel, with shamefacedness and sobriety; not with broided hair, or gold, or pearls, or costly array; But (which becometh women professing godliness) with*

good works."

This must be started early in the life of a girl. If she never wears pants for the first time, she will always wear skirts. If she never wears mini-skirts for the first time, she will always wear skirts of a modest length. In these days of hot pants, mini-skirts, and pant suits, may God give us some old-fashioned mothers and dads who will rear some sweet, feminine ladies for our boys and dress them accordingly.

2.   *Teach her strict obedience.* Other chapters stress the fact that obedience is the most necessary ingredient to be required from the child. This is especially true in the life of a girl, for she must be obedient all of her life. The boy who is obedient to his mother and father will someday become the head of the home; not so for the girl. Whereas the boy is being trained to be a leader, the girl is being trained to be a follower. Hence, obedience is far more important to her, for she must someday transfer it from her parents to her husband.

This means that she should never be allowed to argue at all. She should become submissive and obedient. She must obey immediately, without question, and without argument. The parents who require this have done a big favor for their future son-in-law.

3.   *She should not be allowed to play alone with boys.* The parents should see to it that she plays with other girls. This is important for many reasons. She should play only with toys that are uniquely for girls. This, by all means, should include dolls, doll clothes, housecleaning equipment, dishes, pots and pans, etc. She should participate in sports enough to become coordinated but she should not excel in sports. If later she marries a man who is very athletic, she could become more proficient in some particular sport that he enjoys, but if she becomes an expert in a sport

that is usually associated with men and boys, it could prove embarrassing to her future husband, and for that matter, it could entice her to become more masculine than she ought to be.

4. *Teach her how to be graceful in sitting, walking, etc.* Every mother who has a daughter should be careful to show her how to sit like a lady, walk like a lady, and exhibit propriety and grace in her manners. (Note the chapter on MANNERS.)

5. *Teach her to be an intelligent listener and an articulate conversationalist.* She should read a variety of good books and magazines and have a wide variety of knowledge. It should be obvious to any male with whom she is conversing that she is an intelligent listener and that she can understand and respond to his conversation. She should never seem to know as much as he does (even though she may actually know more) but enough to talk intelligently about his interests and to make him feel that his conversation is falling on receptive ears and an understanding mind. This means that she should learn all she can about everything, especially things that interest men. For example, she should know football, but she should not play it. There is nothing that a man wants any more than to be understood by an intelligent listener.

The wise lady will never "take over" the conversation. She will add just enough to make a valuable contribution and to show her intelligence on the subject, but she will always make her man feel that he is the more knowledgeable. Of course, as a girl like this chooses a man, she will want to choose the kind that is at least her equal, the kind that she will not have to dominate, and the kind whose mind and conversation will always intrigue her. This means that the wise mother will teach her girl not to be a wallflower and not to attempt to get by on beauty alone. She will teach her to be the kind of young lady who has a beautiful spirit and a beautiful soul, one who can communicate, one who is understanding, and one who is quietly articulate in conversation.

Though she should not be a football fanatic she should know enough about football to enjoy watching the game with her boyfriend, fiancé, or husband, if he so chooses. It should be obvious to him that she is enjoying the game and that she is knowledgeable about it, but that he can teach her even more.

6. *Teach her to make her dad feel like a hero.* A young lady that can treat her dad properly is more likely to treat her husband properly. If she makes her dad feel like a man when he is in her presence, she will no doubt make her husband feel like a man when he is in her presence. If the daughter is careful to refill Dad's glass at the table, see to it that he gets the best chair, listen to him intelligently when he talks, participate intelligently, yet meekly in the conversation, she will someday transfer this to her husband and her husband will rise up and call her, "blessed."

7. *Teach her to have the proper heroines.* The mother should be very careful to see to it that the daughter does not idolize Hollywood starlets, female athletes, etc. but rather, feminine, yet successful women like the Biblical characters Hannah and Elisabeth, and characters in history like Susannah Wesley and Elizabeth Barrett Browning. Also point out feminine ladies whose path is crossed by the daughter and lead her to emulate them. It is very important that the young lady, even the girl, look up and idolize the right kind of people.

8. *Teach her not to be too forward to boys.* A young lady should not initiate a correspondence. If she cares for a boy, she may respond to him with courtesy and feminine reserve so as to let him know

she likes him, but she should not be the aggressor, neither should she respond except within the bounds of propriety and right. It certainly is not proper for a young lady to call a young man on the telephone for a social talk, If there is obvious business, it may be done with reluctance, but it should never be done when the call is strictly for social purposes.

9. *Do not show off her talent to others.* As is mentioned elsewhere in this book it is far better for a parent to compliment character than talent. Many children have been ruined because their parents were too proud of them and their performances. This not only hurts the child but it disgusts other adults. In such cases the child receives far too much attention and then wants it for the rest of her life. Hence, she becomes maladjusted. Let her gain her own attention by her performance. Let her attract her own audience by her own ability and opportunities, not by the insistence of a mother or father who is overly proud of a daughter.

10. *Let her do things that enable her to be a necessary help to another who is in the limelight.* This is very important for a young lady. That is why learning to accompany a soloist is good training for a girl. Learning to take dictation is also good training. Both of these things train her to be a necessary helper to someone who is in the limelight. The Bible teaches that a woman is made not for the limelight but to complement and supplement. Proverbs 31:23 says, *"Her husband is known in the gates, when he sitteth among the elders of the land."*

The girl should be taught that her lot in life is to be obedient and helpful to her husband. Hence, if as a girl she can perform supplemental duties that are vital, she will be better equipped to be a well-adjusted lady. It is more important that a young lady be an accompanist on a piano than a concert pianist.

Parents who train their daughter in this manner will someday be called, "blessed," by their son-in-law.

11. *Teach her to pull for her dad.* The wise mother will teach the girl to make a hero of her father and always pull for him. She should pull for him in business and do all she can to help. She should pull for him in any athletic contest and do all she can to cheer him to victory. In everything he does she should stand on the sidelines and root for her dad. She is being taught to root foor the biggest man in her life and to cheer and spur him on to bigger heights. When she is married she will transfer this to her husband and will be a great encouragement to him.

The mother must teach the daughter that when the father is a success the daughter is also a success. She is a very vital part in his success, and as a member of the team she can share the victory and the spoils. When this attitude is properly developed she will feel the same way when she is married. When the husband wins a victory it will be a team victory rather than a victory just for him.

12. *Teach her to plan for a profession but to hope that it will not be needed.* Mothers and fathers should teach their daughters to train for some kind of profession that is always in demand. There is always the possibility that the daughter will never marry or that she will become a widow with children to rear and will not remarry. Because of this she should plan to pursue some profession that will enable her to support herself and her children in any eventuality. She should be taught that if possible, she should not follow this profession when married. This gives her a dependence, if the opportunity arises to be dependent, but an independence if needed. There are many professions that a young lady could pursue such as that of a school teacher, beautician, secretary,

nurse, etc.

13. *Teach her the sanctity of the body.* Teach her that boys should keep their hands off and that her body should be clean in every way. She should care for her body. She should be well groomed and physically clean. Then she should also be moral and virtuous. Talk with her about situations which arise in the lives of most young ladies. Teach her how to handle each situation. Explain to her that that is the reason she should not be in a car alone with a boy. Teach her what to do if improper advances are made. Let her be conscious of the fact that her body is a very sacred thing and should always be treated as the temple of the Holy Spirit.

14. *Teach her to do feminine chores.* As is mentioned elsewhere it is better for a girl to do the dishes than the yard, to wash the pots and pans than the car, to clean the bedroom rather than the garage. She should do the duties that she will do when she is married and a successful mother and wife.

Much stress should be placed on the importance of her working hard. It is not feminine to be lazy. In fact, it is quite feminine to work hard. It is not working hard that makes one unfeminine; it is the doing of masculine tasks. Wise is that mother who teaches her daughter that good hard work is feminine and that the work a woman should do should be that of feminine chores.

15. *Let her be around feminine women.* Teach her to associate with ladies who are feminine. Point them out to her when she is a little girl and tell her they are the ones she should copy and emulate. Let these ladies be those who dress like ladies, talk like ladies, walk with feminine grace, sit with feminine charm. Let these be ladies who are good mothers and who have poise, dedication, chastity, consecration, and spirituality.

16. *Let her baby-sit.* It should be remembered that someday she will no doubt be a mother. She can prepare herself for this and train for it by caring for little ones while she is a teenager. When a girl gets around thirteen, she should become acquainted with taking care of little babies and small children. Her motherly instinct will be developed and nourished. This is very important in preparing her to be a successful and happy mother.

17. *Let her care for younger girls in the family.* Let her dress them, do their hair, wash their faces, etc. Even a girl seven or eight can care for a little sister. She should be encouraged to do so. This will teach her to fulfill responsibilities, to carry the load in the family circly, to work hard, and to prepare herself for motherhood.

18. *Allow her to do no loud shouting or hollering.* In fact, such should not be a part of anyone's household. The business of rearing children can be transacted without shouting or fussing. Especially should this be true in a girl, for the parent is to try in every way to make her quiet, meek and feminine.

19. *With the passing of the years, let her shop more for herself, and if she has younger sisters, let her aid them in doing their shopping.* This will teach her to care for her own person and also for the needs of others.

The most noble goal that parents can set for their daughters is to help them become Christians. The second most noble goal is to lead them to be ladies, for one of the great needs of our generation is Christian ladies. May God use this chapter to make it so.

Chapter Twenty-One

HOW TO MAKE A MAN OUT OF A BOY

My only son, David, is sixteen. God has called him to be a preacher, and he is already preparing for the ministry. A couple of summers ago while David was working as a cowboy at the Bill Rice Ranch, he was asked by Dr. Bill Rice to preach on his local radio broadcast. Several people came to me telling of the blessings they received because of David's sermon; one person especially spoke highly of his radio message and asked me if I would be using David to preach at the First Baptist Church in Hammond. I replied in the negative! He was shocked and asked, "How do you expect to make a preacher out of David if you never let him preach?" My answer was, "I am not trying to make a preacher out of David; I am trying to make a man out of him, for if I can make a man out of him, God can make him a preacher!" We have too many preachers now who are not men! I have spent thousands of hours trying to make a man out of my son. The words that follow will explain how I have tried and the methods I have used.

There is a great need for men of leadership and men of decision in every phase of our American life. The Kinsey report revealed that four per cent of our males over 16 years of age are homosexuals. In California, a sadly misguided preacher found to be a homosexual has founded a church for homosexuals. In the larger cities, clubs for homosexuals have been organized so they can meet regularly together. In our big cities there are homosexual men who live with other men and in a large city recently there was a wedding ceremony which united two men in matrimony. The "Gay" or homosexual community has its own beaches, restaurants, bars, and barber shops; its own tailors, gymnasiums, and apartment houses; its own books, magazines, and periodicals; its own male prostitutes and conventions.

The Wolfinder report says, "Homosexuality between adults in private could no longer be a criminal offense. It is not the law's business." A leading official of the United Church of Canada said, "The church should solemnize marriages between men."

In New York City the Homosexuality League polled 400 homosexuals and asked them, "If you could be cured, would you want to be cured?"

"No," was the answer given by 96% of the homosexuals polled.

Apart from the homosexual problem there is yet a great void in American life. We need men of conviction, discipline, integrity, decision, character, and leadership. Since nothing happens accidentally, if we rear a generation of such men, it must be done in the homes, in the churches, and in the schools, by the parents, pastors, and teachers.

Let us answer the question, "How can I make a man of my boy?"

1. *Dress him like a man.* As soon as his hair gets a bit shaggy, have it cut! It is better that little Johnny start life being masculine than to retain those beautiful ringlets at the age of two. Cut off those ringlets and make him look like a man. From the very first time that he is old enough to wear clothes, dress him like a boy, cut his hair like a boy, and make sure he always looks like a man. Teach him to be around boys that dress like boys. Teach him it is not

Scriptural for a boy or man to have long hair or effeminate tastes in clothing. Read I Corinthians 11:14.

2. *Teach him strict obedience.* He will never be a good leader until he has learned to be an obedient follower, for, to be a leader, one must know the heartbeat of the follower so he will know how to handle followers. Let him know the rules; state them plainly so he knows what they are. Tell him exactly what the penalty will be if he breaks a rule. Define the crime and the punishment so he knows before he commits it whether it will be worth it or not. Always make the punishment so great that the committing of the crime will not be worth it. If I were a boy eighteen years of age and my dad said to me, "You get home by 11:00 o'clock tonight; I'm going to fuss at you if you don't!" I might be tempted to spend an extra half hour with my girlfriend and take Dad's scolding. However, if my dad were to take the car away from me for a month if I were late returning home, I would stop to realize that any time I arrived home late I would be trading a few minutes with my girlfriend for a whole month of dates, and that is not a good bargain! Make the punishment so uncomfortable that it will not be worth it to break the rules. Make your son live by strict discipline and obedience. Teach him to say "Yes, sir" and "Yes, ma'am" and "No, sir" and "No, ma'am."

3. *Punish him immediately and properly.* Do not jerk him up and call him a little brat. Take him to his room, make him sit down, tell him what he did wrong, tell him what you are going to do, then do it and tell him why you did it. Make a big ordeal out of it. Make the punishment private, but make it immediate, proper, and plain.

4. *Make him fulfill all obligations.* When my boy was three and four years of age I started teaching him

to pay his bills promptly and to fulfill his obligations completely. I would ask him, "Son, if a debt is due on the first of the month, when are you going to pay it?"

He would say, "On the first of the month."

Then I would ask, "Son, if an emergency arises and you cannot meet your obligation, what are you supposed to do?"

He would then reply, "I am supposed to go to the person I owe, shake his hand, look him in the eye, and have an understanding as to what can be done."

What the American male needs is honor, just plain, old, downright honor. We need men of the old school who sat straight in their chairs and led with firmness and love. When the kids walked in they felt like they were before a Supreme Court Justice. Maybe they didn't like him then or understand him, but later they rose up and called him, "blessed."

He was of the old school—a man who was very careful about going in debt, a man whose word was as good as his signature, a man who was upright, honest, aboveboard, and who helped his neighbor when he was in trouble. Teach your boy that promptness is a part of character. Teach him to take care of his obligations properly.

This is one of the things that is killing fundamentalism today. We have some shiftless, dirty, irresponsible, lackadaisical, sluggards who are fundamentalists that refuse to pay their debts, take care of their property, keep their word, press their pants, and shine their shoes. They know nothing of courtesy, etiquette, ethics and are bereft of integrity, honest, decency, and honor. Let this not be true in the life of your son.

5. *Teach him physical coordination.* I do not mean that he has to be a great athlete, but his body should be coordinated. Insist that he participate in

athletics. It is a grave danger for a boy to be indoors too much and grow up not knowing how to coordinate his body properly.

6. *Teach him to want to win.* We have stressed to our children, "Be a good loser, be a good loser, be a good loser," until we have rubbed this good loser bit in the ground! I taught my boy to play to win. We have bragged on good losers until our boys have received more rewards for losing gracefully than winning properly. The result has been that we now have a nation of young people who do not want to fight for their country and who are willing to let the strongest nation on earth bow down in shame before a little nation like North Vietnam. It is tragic, but true, that I know hundreds of men who couldn't beat their wives at Chinese checkers. Junior has been taught to be a good loser; he has been rewarded for being a good loser, so winning becomes less and less important.

I was approached by a pastor in Rockford, Illinois. He was somewhat effeminate and less than a man. He came to me and with his dainty voice he said, "Dr. Hyles, can I ask you a question? You strike me as being a very poor loser. Is that true?" I looked at him, paused a moment, and answered, "Don't know . . . I ain't never lost!"

If you are going to make a man of your boy, teach him to be a winner. Yes, he must accept loss gracefully, but he should never enjoy losing. This is where we get our General MacArthurs. This is how Billy Sundays are made. Teach your boy to want to win.

7. *Make him play with boys and with boys' toys and games.* Let him play with guns, cars, baseballs, basketballs, and footballs. As soon as I could I taught my boy to play baseball and football. When he was about thirteen I bought him an air rifle. When he was

fifteen I bought him a .22 rifle. Invariably, when someone admits to me he is a homosexual he relates that he played a lot with girls and participated in feminine activities.

8. *Compliment character, not talent.* Never has David stood up on the hearth at home to sing a song for applause. I have never applauded him for his talent, but many times I have applauded him because he obeyed. Compliment his character, not his talent. It will make a better man of him.

9. *Do not keep him "under your thumb."* Let him spend the night with other boys (good Christian boys). Send him off to camp in the summertime, even when he is seven or eight years of age. Let him learn how to kill a snake, put frogs in his pocket, tie a knot, and build a fire. Let him get blisters on his feet and at an early age let him start doing what men ought to do.

If the music director dosen't choose him for a singing group, don't be the kind of parent that complains in defense of the boy's talent. If care is not taken, you will rear a boy that expects you to come to his rescue and bail him out every time he is in trouble. If he is going to be a man someday, he must start in childhood having some responsibilities, some discomforts, and some manly obligations. He will not jump from being a little boy into being a man; it is a gradual process. Be sure this natural process is allowed to develop.

10. *Always stand for proper authority.* Not long ago one of my staff members came to me complaining that his boy was disciplined too heavily by his church choir director. I lovingly warned my staff member that he should thank God that his boy was being disciplined. If the punishment is too severe, it will still be a lot better for him than for the boy to learn that his dad will not take his side over proper

authority.

One of our finest boys who is going to be a preacher came to my office the other night and said, "Brother Hyles, my teacher is persecuting me."

"Why?" I asked.

He said, "I come to church on Wednesday nights and am so busy in activities that I don't get all my homework done, and my school teacher is going to give me a bad grade for that."

"She ought to," I said.

"Well," he said, "I have been coming to church faithfully."

I said, "Okay, then, study when you are at home, but don't come to me because your grade is bad when you don't do your work." The boy who is going to become a real man must learn to respect authority.

11. *Teach him to defend himself.* Yes, you read it right. Teach him self-defense. Yes, you still read it right. Teach him how to fight. Teach him to be rugged enough to defend his own own, his home, his loved ones, and his friends.

When David was just five years of age, I bought him a pair of boxing gloves. In fact, I bought one pair for David and one pair for the big boy across the street. I got them together and let them box. The boy punched David in the nose; David wanted to quit, but I wouldn't let him. I was going to teach him how to defend himself, how to be a man—physically a man, emotionally a man, mentally a man, and spiritually a man. He learned to fight until now he can protect his sisters.

One day when David was about nine I looked out through the upstairs window and saw him across the street straddling a little fellow and beating him up. He was hitting him right in the face until blood was coming. I ran down the stairs, out the door, across the street and pulled him off. "Son, what in the world are you doing?" I said.

He looked up with quivering lips and with anger in his eyes said, "Dad, he was calling my sister (Linda) a dirty name."

I said, "Then get back on him and let him have it!" When I walked away he was back on him again beating him up. God pity this weak-kneed generation which stands for nothing, fights for nothing, and dies for nothing.

12. *Teach him to shop alone.* By the time he is around ten or eleven years of age let him shop by himself for a few things. There is nothing any more disgusting than to see a big eighteen-year-old boy trying on pants at the men's shop with his little mother breathing down his neck. Maybe he won't match his socks exactly with his tie, but I would rather he be a man than to have matching tie and socks. Now, to be sure, my preference is that he be both proper and a man.

The other day I saw a big six-foot, two-inch eighteen-year-old boy walking in a store beside his five-foot, four-inch mother. The salesman asked, "What size do you wear, son?"

His mother said, "He wears size 42."

The salesman asked, "Son, do you want something single-breasted or double-breasted?"

The mother replied, "He wants single-breasted."

There were two words I would like to have used to that lady. The first one is "shut" and the second, "up." Mothers, let your boys become men. One of these days he will grow up and have to marry a mother instead of a wife. His wife will have to pick out every tie he wears, lay it on the bed every morning, and burp him before he goes to bed at night. What you will have is a grown son who will have to marry a mother or he won't be happy. You are robbing some lady of having a man for a husband

and you are robbing your boy of ever having a chance to be a man. If he is going to be a man of decision someday, let him make some decisions now. He is not going to lead a big corporation if he cannot buy his own tie by the time he is old enough to make the football team.

At a very early age a boy should start making his own decisions. Now, to be sure, there should be governing and overseeing, and there should be limits, but if he is someday going to make decisions that are going to affect a great church, city, nation, or corporation, he must be taught while a little child to make the decisions about what socks he is going to wear.

13. *Talk to him like a man.* Some mothers say to their sixteen-year-old boy, "Take the garbage out, baby," "Bye-bye, sweetheart," "Good morning precious," "Be sure you are back on time, sugar baby," or "Be careful, honey doll." Talk to him like a man! When he becomes a teenager, don't kiss him in public unless he initiates it.

No teenage boy ever comes into my office and is treated anything less than a man to man. The teenage boys walk in my office like men, they dress like men, they shake my hand like men, they look me in the eye and talk to me like men, and they say, "Yes, sir'" and "No, sir" like gentlemen. Don't treat the boy like a baby if you want him someday to be a man.

14. *Give him work, authority, and responsibility.* Be sure he knows how to work (for that matter, I think a boy should know how to take suffering, pain and punishment). That is one reason I like sports. When David was just five years old I got a baseball, went out in the yard, knocked him grounders, and gave him a quarter for every one he could catch. He didn't make a single quarter. I hit them too hard. They bounced up and hit him in the chest, in the

nose, in the head, and in the shoulder. He came in bruised and broken, but more a man.

Give your boy responsibility. Give him something to do as regular work and make him responsible for it. Don't breathe down his neck. Teach him to have initiative.

One of the reasons ladies ofttimes turn out to be better leaders than men is that city life is conducive to this. There are not many chores for boys to do like milking the cow, chopping the wood, etc. There are chores for the girls. What happens? Boys grow up without any chores, no milking cows, no feeding pigs, no gathering eggs, no chores like we had on the farm or at the edge of town. Girls, however, can iron, keep house, cook, wash and dry the dishes. Hence, they are taught initiative, whereas the boys find few masculine duties to perform. Hence, the parent must work hard to find masculine-type duties.

I never let my boy do feminine chores. The dish washing has been done by the girls. He does no ironing, etc. He must keep his room clean and tidy, but his chores have been masculine chores such as cleaning the basement, taking out the garbage, having an afternoon job, moving the yard, etc.

A few years ago Dr. Bill Rice wrote me and said, "Dr. Hyles, would David like to have a pony?" I thought, "Where in the world are we going to keep a pony?" Well, I said we would find some place. We went to a neighbor who has a big back yard and a little shed. We borrowed his shed. Yes, right in the city we had a pony. At night the phone would ring and it would be the police department calling, "Do you have a horse? It is running down Schreiber Street." After a while every time the phone would ring at night I would pick it up and say, "Where is the horse now?"

I told David, "Son, you wanted the horse, you

have to feed him." David would get up in the morning, trudge through the snow in sub-zero weather, carry a water bucket in one hand and a bag of feed in the others, and go feed the horse. He learned to ride the horse even though the horse spent more time at the police station than he did in the shed. David owned one of the few ponies in America who had a police record.

A boy needs responsibility; he also needs to assume authority. Give him that responsibility and authority and teach him to work.

15. *Do not make a mold for your boy.* If you are a lawyer, don't decide before he is born that he is going to be a lawyer. If you are a preacher, let your son decide what God wants him to do. Don't let him think you will be disappointed if he is not what he thinks you want him to be. Now everyone knows that I would like for David to be a preacher, but I will let God decide that. If David becomes an honest man of character and becomes the best garbage collector in Hammond, his dad will be proud of him. It would be wrong for me to make a mold for him.

16. *Give him opportunities to lead.* Though David is younger than my oldest daughter I have always preferred to leave him in charge of the family. When I am away on a trip, it is understood that David does the manly chores. He has learned to be protective of his sisters and the house. The family feels as safe when he is there as when I am there. He has been taught and trained to be physically capable as well as emotionally capable.

17. *Teach him to have proper heroes.* This is one of the greatest things my mother ever did for me. She pointed to men whom I could emulate and who could be my heroes. I tried to become like those men. I will be eternally grateful for the fact that my mother gave me heroes. This is one reason why parents should

choose a church which has a masculine pastor.
Mothers and dads should be able to say to their sons,
"Grow up and be like your pastor," without having
to fear that he will be effeminate. It is wise for the
parents to choose older boys who are gentlemen and
yet real men and set them as examples for boys.
Proper athletic heroes, Sunday school teachers, manly
pastors, and older boys could be chosen.

David and I have been buddies form his infancy.
He always waits for me after church and rides home
with me. Since I have duties to perform I always
come home later than the rest of the family, but
David has always waited for me. As a little boy four
or five, he wanted to wait for Daddy. Now as a
teenage boy on the basketball team, he still wants to
wait for Dad. For years I drove him home and now he
drives me home.

Recently David had to wait two and a half hours
on Sunday evening for his dad. When we got home
someone asked him why he didn't come home earlier
with the rest of the family. He replied that he wanted
to wait for his dad. Then they asked him, "What did
you do for two and a half hours alone out in the
hall?"

David stood up and with masculine physique and
presentation he said, "I will tell you what I did for
that two and a half hours alone in the hall: I walked
up and down the hallway realizing how many people
would love to wait two and a half hours to get to ride
home with Dr. Jack Hyles, and I thanked God that I
have the privilege."

Nearly seventeen years ago I got on my knees over
the body of my only son and prayed for God to make
him a man. I never prayed that he would be a
preacher; I prayed he would be a man, a Christian man
with integrity, discipline, leadership, ability, courtesy,
gentleness, strength and honor; yes, in every way, a real

man. I have tried now for almost seventeen years to help him become a man. I think he will, I believe I am now ending that work that I sent out to do that day. I think I have about made, with God's help, a man out of a boy.

Chapter Twenty-Two

HOW TO REAR A TEENAGER

Mark Twain once said that when a child becomes a teenager he should be put in a box and locked up. A hole should be drilled in the box just big enough for air to get through so the teenager can breathe. When he becomes seventeen, the parents should plug up the hole! This, of course, is not true of a teenager who is reared by wise parents who carefully plan their relationship with him. When a child becomes a teenager he is no more a child and should no longer be treated as a child; he should be treated as a teenager. He is coming toward the end of his years at home. Many cords that have bound him to his parents will soon be broken. He is busily engaged in more outside activities than ever before. He no longer needs his parents in the same ways he has needed them in childhood. He is physically, mentally, and emotionally becoming an adult. During these brief years in "no man's land" when he is neither a child nor an adult he must not be treated as he has been. His needs are unique. If they are properly met, these needs can be used to strengthen the teenager's relationship with his parents and strengthen the tie that binds them.

This chapter deals with those unique and peculiar methods that should be used by the parent during these important years. No attempt at continuity will be made. There will simply be presented some unrelated observations that have come from over a quarter of a century of counseling with teenagers.

1. *Do not yield to the temptation to be simply his*

buddy. It is true that as a child grows older he has more
things in common with his parents. He should not,
however, be led to feel he is their equal. There should
still be a reverential fear and complete obedience. He
should still address his parents by their proper titles,
and though the conversations between parent and
teenager will be more adult-like it should not be
allowed to breed over-familiarity.

   2.   *Do not force conversation but keep the lines of
communication open.* A teenager wants to know that
Mom and Dad are present and interested. He wants to
know that they are available at all times when he
needs their counsel. He does not, however, want them
to force conversation. Perhaps the young girl has
become interested in a fine Christian boy in the
church but is somewhat timid about it. She should
feel that Mom and Dad are interested and will give
her a sympathetic ear and wise counsel if it is sought.
She should feel that the lines of communication are
open, but that she has the right to initiate such a
conversation. In other words, within bounds, the
teenager should have more privacy than a child. This
does not mean he has a right to do wrong if he so
chooses, but that within the realm of right he has
more room to move around.
   3.   *Always take seriously his problems.* The
problems may seem juvenile and humorous to the
parent, but they are very serious to the teenager. The
wise parent will not use such statements as "You'll
outgrow that," "That's just puppy love," "We all go
through that stage," "I was like that when I was a
kid," etc. Many teenagers have come to my office
with problems, and when I asked them why they did
not discuss their problem with Mom and Dad they
answered, "They would just laugh at me," "They
wouldn't think it was important enough," etc. If a

subject is serious to the teenager, it should be serious
to the parent. He should not be timid about his
problems, his dates, or his activities. If he cannot
receive a sympathetic and conscientious ear at home,
he will seek it elsewhere. This one of the main reasons
why teenagers often say, "I just can't talk to my
mom and dad."

4. *Do not take away good in order to punish the
teenager.* Do not deprive him of doing the good that
he does in order to punish him for doing bad. Many
parents unwisely punish by forbidding attendance at
the teenage prayer band, teenage soul winning, or
other church-centered youth activity. The fact that
he has done something wrong means that he needs
more than ever these avenues of spiritual growth. He
should be punished by being deprived of something
pleasant to him, but not of his opportunity to serve
the Lord.

5. *Do not use the doing of a good task as
punishment.* It does not seem wise for a parent to
punish a girl by making her do the dishes or punishing
a boy by making him mow the yard. Distaste is
created toward the doing of good. The doing of the
dishes becomes something bad which is used by Mom
for punishment. It would be much better to start in
early childhood and reward a child for being good by
allowing her to do the dishes as a reward. Hence,
work becomes honorable and dignified instead of
distasteful punishment.

6. *Never shout or scream at a teenager.* Much
more can be done with frankness and firmness. The
parent who screams at his teenager will soon find him
withdrawing, and the line of communication will be
broken.

7. *Seek the teenager's counsel on matters.* Talk
over serious things with him. His advice will not
always be wise and should not always be used, but it

should be considered. By so doing the parent is not only satisfying the inner desire in the heart of the young person to be accepted as more mature, he is also helping prepare him for the decisions of adult life.

In writing this book I have often sought the counsel of my children. This has not only enabled me to gather information helpful to others, but it has also aided the children in realizing their importance to Dad. The parent and child should have periodic serious discussions when fathers can seek advice concerning matters at work and mothers can receive counsel concerning homemaking. It should be repeated that the decision making should be in the hands of the parents, not the teenagers, but their counsel should be seriously sought and considered.

8. *Show him the logic behind certain decisions.* When he asks for something that requires a "no" answer, explain to him in detail whey he was deprived of his request. Do not allow him the extravagance of arguing or complaining, but do allow him the privilege of knowing why. He may not always agree with your logic, but it will allow him to know that there was logic behind your decision, and it will also help him as he rears his own children.

9. *Teach him teamwork.* It is far better for the teenager to be part of a winning team than to achieve for himself a winning performance. I would prefer my boy to run on a relay team than to run the 100-yard dash. I would prefer him to be a member of a winning basketball team than to win a golf championship. I would rather he win a tennis match by playing doubles rather than singles.

Of course, there are children and young people who have developed an inferiority complex and need individual achievement. However, a proper balance should be sought and every child should be taught teamwork.

When a child shows tendencies toward selfishness, by all means he should be led into group activity. Suppose, for example, that a teenage lad is selfish and never pulls for others. If he plays on a team, then in order to pull for victory he must pull for others, for in pulling for others he is pulling for himself. If this is done long enough and often enough, he will no doubt subconsciously transfer this desire for their success as his team members to their own individual efforts, for he has formed the habit of pulling for them. An unselfish desire for their success has replaced a selfish desire for team victory.

10. *Do not allow the teenager's desire for privacy to develop into an obsession for secrecy.* The natural withdrawal from Mom and Dad is accelerated during the teen years. The door that was once wide open is now shut and soon will be locked. The little wide-eyed girl who used to want to go to the store with Dad now wants to stay at home. Though this desire for privacy should be honored, it should not be allowed to develop into secrecy. If the teen has his own room, let him retreat into its privacy, but insist that the door usually be kept open. When on occasion the door is shut (and there should be such occasions) do not allow it to be locked. He should realize that though he is growing older and needs more privacy, that privacy should be earned and when it becomes secrecy, he has forfeited his right to privacy.

There may be times when the youth will want to retire to his own room and listen to the radio. He should not be allowed to do so with the use of ear plugs. Many Christian parents do not realize that their youngsters are listening to music that is detrimental to their development.

It is best that when a teenager talks on the telephone he do so in some place that is only semiprivate. He should not be allowed the luxury of having a phone in his own room. Though the family should not snoop while he is talking on the phone, they should nevertheless feel free to carry on the regular routine of living even though this might necessitate an occasional passing through the room or the hallway where he is talking. He should not be allowed to dominate the telephone and tie it up for long periods of time. Such practices breed selfishness, idleness and secrecy.

When at all possible the teen's room should be near the center of activity. It is best that his room not be the one at the end of the hall where no one else ever passes. It is best for his to be nearer the center of the house. This will not take away his privacy, but it will prevent his secrecy. There is a temptation on the part of many parents to go the extreme by allowing the child to be aloof from the rest of the family. On the other extreme is the parent who adopts gestapo tactics of investigation. Both are dangerous. The wise parent will certainly respect the child's desire for privacy as this desire is a normal part of the development of the teen years. He will, however, let the child know that this privacy is earned and will be taken away when it becomes secrecy.

11. *Teach him appropriate and proper behavior toward the opposite sex.* With the coming of the teen years there comes also an awareness of the opposite sex and its attrativeness. This is normal and should not be discouraged. During these years, however, careful training should be given to the child concerning dating and the developing of his relationship to this new gender he is beginning to notice.

(1) *Teach him from childhood not to date unconverted people.* Since the Bible forbids the Christian to marry an unconverted person, the wise

parent will instill in the mind of his child the danger of even having a date with one who in unsaved. I have taught the teenagers in our church not to date someone who would not meet the spiritual qualifications they would want to find in their mates.

(2) *Use wisdom in determining the age for a child to begin dating.* It seems unwise for a pre-teen to have any other relationship with a member of the opposite sex than that of having a boyfriend or girlfriend at school, etc. Then during the early teens perhaps the parent should allow them to sit together in church and in other public meetings. They should not, however, be allowed to sit near the back of the auditorium, and at this age, they should always be within seeing distance of their parents. At first it would be wise for them to sit with the parents, and then later perhaps in some conspicuous place, but never in a corner, in the back, or in the balcony. (At the First Baptist Church of Hammond we allow no teenager to sit in the balcony unless he is accompanied by an adult.)

As the middle or older teen years approach the parent should carefully observe the teenager so as to discern whether he should be allowed to have an actual date in a car, and even then he should never be alone in a car with a member of the opposite sex. One of the most dangerous things a parent can do is allow his child to go unchaperoned on a single date.

Double dating should be permitted to more mature teenagers only when the two boys are in the car before either girl is called for, and both girls are delivered home before either boy has left the car. Even then the parents should know and approve each member of the party.

(3) *The parent should warn the teenager of the dangers of going steady.* There is only so much ground to cover between the first date and marriage.

If too much of this territory is covered before the couple is ready for marriage, there is a grave danger present. When a relationship develops too rapidly so as to make the next step that of marriage, a couple must then either marry or break up. This causes many people to break up permanently who otherwise would have married each other. If a teenager really cares for another, he must wisely space the steps before marriage so as to arrive at his destination (the marriage altar) at the same time emotionally, mentally, physically, and for that matter, financially. The parent should warn the teenager that there are more couples who do not get married because of going steady as teenagers than there are who do marry because they decided to go steady. Hence, going steady will probably come nearer keeping the teenager from marrying the one for whom he is fond, rather than causing him to marry her.

Then too, the teen should be warned that the desire to go steady is usually caused by an inferiority complex. One feels insecure and thinks his own personality is unable to hold the affection of the one to whom he is attracted, so he makes a contract of some sort with her so that what he is unable to do the contract will do. If a couple truly loves each other, they will not need to go steady. If they do not love each other, they should not go steady.

(4) *Boys should not be allowed to drop in unannounced to see a girl*. The young man should have an appointment with the young lady or he should not come. This appointment should always be approved by a least one of the parents. Casual dropping in and hanging around is dangerous and in poor taste. Of course, this is even more true for a young lady. It is even in poor taste for a young lady to call a boy on the telephone unless there is business to transact. A social phone call should always be

initiated by the young man. When he comes to see the young lady it should be by appointment only with the full knowledge and approval of the parents.

(5) *The parent should always know where the teenager is and what he is doing.* For example, if he is playing miniature golf, the parent should know at what miniature golf course he is playing, approximately how long he will be there, where he will go when he finishes, and what time he will be home. The parent should approve every place and activity.

Of course, there should be certain places that are off limits. Clear and detailed instructions should be given to the young people concerning these places.

If for some reason the plans for the evening have to be altered, the teen should call his parents and explain what has happened and what the alternate plans are. These plans should be approved by the parent. Any change of plans or activities should be reported to the parent immediately by telephone.

(6) *The parent should teach the young person dating etiquette.* Each teenager should know how to behave properly and appropriately while in the presence of a member of the oppisite sex and especially on a date. The boy should be taught how to open a door for the young lady. The girl should be taught to step aside and allow him to do so. The boy should be taught to open the car door for his date and the girl should be taught to wait until he does so. A girl should be taught not to sit too close to a boy. The boy should be taught to keep his hands off of her! Both should be warned against embracing, kissing, etc.

(7) *Teenagers should be taught the proper way to close a date.* Stress should be given to getting her home on time and having a prayer of thanksgiving together for the good time enjoyed. The girl should

then in good taste tell the young man that she had a good time, and he should then politely escort her to the door, speak an expressive word if he so desires, and in a mannerly and gentlemanly way, say, "Good night."

May God help us to lead our children wisely through these crucial days when they are in "no man's land" — too old to be children and too young to be adults, so that we will not have to "plug up the hole in the box."

Chapter Twenty-Three

FIFTEEN MINUTES IN ROYALTY

By David Hyles

(Sceptics sometimes remark that disciplining a child and rearing him according to the Bible will make him grow up to hate his parents. Let such sceptics read the following article written by David when he was sixteen. The article was not written for a school assignment or because of any compulsion. It was written simply to express the spontaneous feelings of a sixteen-year-old boy who loves his dad. The article is printed just as it was written, with no proofreading editing changing of spelling of punctuation.)

—Dr. Jack Hyles

All alone I stood in the lobby of the church on a cold dark Sunday nite. Everyone else had left long ago, yet I remained waiting. My father was the pastor, and was again late because of a conference. Every Sunday nite and Wednesday nite I remembered I had waited for him.

It was getting later, and the janitors had all gone home. I shared the building with no one.

Discouraged and a bit angry I began to walk alone through the building. I wondered why I should wait so long just for a fifteen-minute ride home.

Walking past a nursery I looked in and saw bed after bed. I began to dream of a day when maybe I would have a little baby of my own. Would there be a church where I would feel safe to leave my child? Here the nurseries were clean and the babysitters dedicated Christians.

Someday I would have my own child, and he would grow. As he grew I would want him to be taught to obey. I walked past the beginner and primary departments. So many little children came there to be told about Jesus and right and wrong. Would my child have the same?

And as my child grew to be a junior, a junior higher, and even a high schooler, would there be a place like this which stressed discipline and morals—a place which would lead my child toward God's will?

Suddenly I realized what a great place this was, and my father was its pastor. People all over the world looked at our church with envy and respect. Hundreds of preachers came here to be taught how to build similar churches.

Many hours were spent without my father at home. He travels over 100,000 miles a year speaking to thousands of people. Why? Because he wanted to have churches everywhere.

People traveled many miles just to hear my father speak. He was a widely-read author and speaker, a nationwide radio speaker, a world-traveling conference speaker, a leader of pastors, and a great man.

Many people would stay up all night just to be able to talk to him for five minutes. Hundreds of people cherish the day they simply met him and shook his hand. Night and day he works and tries to help people.

Out he walked as I sat in the car alone. He opened the door, and got in. "Hi, doc," he said, "how's school coming?"

Away we drove together, talking about sports, church, school, and anything else that came up.

With Dr. Jack Hyles, my father, next to me, I spent fifteen minutes in royalty.

(David never intended for his dad to see the above article and to this day he has no idea that it is being published. His dad discovered the article quite by accident)

Blue Denim

and

Lace

Dr. Jack Hyles

Here is an exciting book for young people and parents. Many teenagers read a chapter each day from BLUE DENIM AND LACE. The book deals with character building and the philosophies that build integrity, decency, chastity, and charcter. Every teenager should read the chapters entitled, "For Sale," "Dangers of Success," "The Body," "Work," "So You Are Out of God's Will," "A Good Name," "Education," "The Christian's Cabinet," "Daniel's Spirit," and "How You Look at Your Life." Every parent should read the chapters entitled, "Rearing Children," "Strength and Beauty," "Perfect Love," "How High Are Your Valleys?" "Holy Places and Holy Days," "Preparedness or Perplexities," "Premature Nostalgia," "Deepening Relationships," and "When Time is No Longer." These are just a few of the 49 chapters covering 175 big pages. Order from Hyles Publications, 523 Sibley Street, Hammond, Indiana 46320.